The Cruise
of
Luna Quest

W. Eric Faber

Melrose Books Ltd

Published by

**MELROSE
BOOKS**

An Imprint of Melrose Press Limited
St Thomas Place, Ely
Cambridgeshire
CB7 4GG, UK
www.melrosebooks.com

FIRST EDITION

Copyright © W. Eric Faber 2011

The Author asserts his moral right to
be identified as the author of this work

Cover designed by Hannah Belcher
Photograph on cover by Marion Faber

ISBN 978 1 907732 35 5

Printed and bound in Great Britain by:
CPI Group (UK) Ltd, Croydon, CR0 4YY

FSC
www.fsc.org
MIX
Paper from
responsible sources
FSC® C013604

I dedicate this book to all sailing-boat enthusiasts whose aspirations lie beyond the horizon.

Contents

About the Author

William Eric Faber was born in Hilversum, Holland in 1943, the youngest of three children, of an English mother and a Dutch father. In Holland he developed his passion for boats from an early age, designing and building model boats, learning to sail on the Dutch lakes and racing a variety of dinghies. At the age of eighteen he won the first national prize for designing and building a 6-foot ketch model boat. With a friend he put together a Hornet dinghy from kit form, which they raced around many of the lakes in Holland. They were national champions in 1965 and were sent to Poland the following year to represent their country in the World Championships. Eric had always thought he wanted to become a boat builder, but his father urged him against that trade. After Grammar School he read English in Amsterdam, which together with his passion for boating and sailing brought him over to England in 1968. Having proved his father right with a false start in the boating industry on the East Coast, a Dutch bank in the City of London offered him employment as a trainee. However, he did not feel the training challenged him enough and to make better use of his linguistic skills he went to work for City stockbrokers to cover the European markets. During this ostensibly prosperous period, a devastating secondary banking crisis developed that saw many banks and stockbrokers go bust, including the firm he worked for. With his stockbroking career coming to an abrupt end, he went back to banking where the Chase Manhattan Bank took him onto their credit-training programme. The many reorganisations that the bank went through gave Eric the opportunity to seek employment with a German bank in the City of London from where he retired in 2004. The daily commute to Liverpool Street Station, an hour each way, allowed him time to read extensively and build a maritime library. The more he read, the keener he became to sail across the oceans in the footsteps of Sir Alec Rose, Sir Francis Chichester, Bernard Moitessier and dozens of other sailors. Although he had it in mind to retire at the age of sixty-three and put his aspiration into action if circumstances allowed, an early retirement opportunity came along when he was sixty-one. Eric and his wife, Marion, have three daughters, a son and five grandchildren. He and his wife live near Saffron Walden in Essex.

Foreword

People's urge to challenge themselves is a constant factor throughout their lives. Boys test their strength, young men test new horizons and older people are tested daily by seemingly insurmountable problems. If it were not for this urge, we would not have the development in industry, commerce, science and technology that we can witness all around the world. Many of us, however, may never have the opportunity to test ourselves in rising to challenges that others seem to have. We are often employed in a structure where different demands are made on us, where we have responsibilities and accountability, where career ambition may have supplanted our aspirations to find our own ultimate challenge. If we are lucky enough to have recognised in ourselves where that ultimate challenge lies, then with interest and enthusiasm we venture out on a road of exploration to find it.

Often we do not rate ourselves competent or brave enough to rise to the ultimate challenge: we believe we are not up to it. True, we cannot all be like Amy Johnson or Mr Bleriot who flew across the Channel in 1909, or Ellen McArthur, who set a new world record sailing solo around the world, but in every challenge a degree of daring is needed, perhaps even recklessness. We weigh them in the scales against care, caution and knowledge, but given as much knowledge and care as we can gather, the degree of daring required may not be enough to launch ourselves into the ultimate challenge. Words of encouragement or a helping hand will go a long way to get us over the hurdle of a lack of confidence.

Sailing is a pursuit like no other. It requires not just skill and a little daring; it requires knowledge and an understanding of the earth's forces and weather patterns. And there are varying levels of challenge on entry into the sport. A child in a Topper dinghy will have the knowledge, the confidence and the protection of his parents or sailing club. A race around the marker buoys will have the committee boat on standby. The fleet racing around the Isle of Wight or the Fastnet Rock will have the benefit of the rescue services to call on, but ocean cruising or racing is in a class of its own. Whereas an ocean race may count fifty boats at the same time on the start line, a day's sailing into the ocean will have spread the fleet sufficiently apart to make each participant feel they are bereft of all human life other than that of the crew, if there is one. Every challenge that presents itself on the high seas has to be dealt with directly for the ocean shows no sympathy and waits for no man. Any failure of anything onboard, however small, could escalate into disaster. Gear failure is a frequent challenge and health failure sets off a chain of consequential challenges. Therefore, before a skipper sets off from his home port, he will have tested the boat, every bit of equipment, checked the medical supplies, the food stores and made provisions for his family and paper work at home.

At World Cruising Club, these challenges are well understood and guidance is provided. There is even a forum for sailors to discuss their worries and ambitions organised by World Cruising Club. Since Sir Francis Chichester, Sir Alec Rose and Sir Robin Knox Johnston made us all believe that we in our GRP boats are much safer than they were in their wooden boats, that our sailing gear is far superior, that our navigation equipment is more accurate and that our communication equipment is reliable, would-be ocean sailors have been waking up to their ultimate challenge. Protected by the knowledge of their superior equipment and the monitoring and tracking qualities offered by World Cruising Club, their numbers have grown substantially since those early years. Of course, the crossing of the Atlantic to the Caribbean islands is undertaken at a time of the year when the hurricanes are out of the way and the trade winds can be expected to fill the sails. The idea that hundreds of yachts take part in the Atlantic Rally for Cruisers also provides the would-be ocean sailor with a degree of reassurance. There is never a yacht so far away that it cannot provide assistance within a day's sail. In 2011 over 250 yachts took part. In 2010 their number was 230. Registration lists were closed earlier than in previous years, such is the demand.

The Atlantic Rally for Cruisers held for Eric Faber a mighty appeal to give vent to his long-held ambition to face his ultimate challenge. After 40 years of employment, he sold his little boat, *Sally*, a 23'6" wooden sloop built in 1934 as soon as he retired in 2004 at the age of 61 to buy instead a Rival 38. His new yacht lay in Turkey and not having had any ocean sailing experience before, he considered that crossing the Mediterranean would be an ideal practice ground. In 2005 he made his boat ready in Turkey to undertake the challenge to cross over to the South Coast of France where he felt he could reliably prepare her for participation in the 2006 Atlantic Rally for Cruisers. World Cruising Club sets down a range of criteria that each boat, skipper and crew must achieve before being allowed to set sail. These stringent criteria give the owner, skipper and crew a warm feeling that they have a master of considerable experience who sets the standards. Having completed all the work required, he set sail along the coast of Spain in 2006 to make Gibraltar and then undertook the week's non-stop sail to the Canary Islands where World Cruising Club has an office in Las Palmas from where the start of the Rally is coordinated and managed. There is always great excitement in the weeks leading up to the start of the Rally at the end of November. Every day yachts arrive from all over Europe, parties are held, lectures given, safety checks carried out and local shops emptied of provisions.

World Cruising Club offers many other rallies including one for the return from the Caribbean to Europe. Sometimes skippers feel sufficiently confident to participate in the World ARC going on from the Caribbean through the Panama Canal and beyond. Whatever a skipper's ambition, World Cruising Club gives him a helping hand just enough for confidence levels to weigh more than caution and daring. May this book serve as an inspiration to other would-be sailors who wish to venture upon the oceans.

Andrew Bishop, World Cruising Club

PART 1

A DREAM COME TRUE

Chapter 1

Early beginnings

In 1981, at my wife's suggestion, I purchased my first boat, a twenty-three-and-a-half-foot wooden sloop built in 1934 called *Sally*. She was a Lymington-L Class, designed by Laurent Giles. She had a very tall wooden mast, placed well forward and a massively long boom. The configuration left insufficient room for a decent foresail, with the result that she sailed well before the wind but with untenable weather helm on the wind. She had a two-stroke two-cylinder cast-iron Stuart Turner petrol engine fitted twenty years into her life, but the sternpost was too slender to take the propeller directly aft so the engine was fitted diagonally with the propeller protruding through the hull on her port side. She had a permanent list to port side, not because of the propeller but because of the elementary way wooden boats were built in the 1930s. The heavy 180kg engine caused her to sit rather lower on her haunches than the designers had intended. To compensate for her odd looks, I had weighed her down in the bow by fitting four lead pigs as far forward as I could manage. I had also fitted two lead pigs to the starboard side to make her sit up straight and disguise her poor posture. Great clouds of blue and black smoke would billow from her exhaust for the first five minutes, which always embarrassed me, especially as people had become sometimes too environmentally friendly for my liking from the 1990s onward. Luckily, once the engine ran at full throttle, the smoke became less visible and my feelings of guilt would subside with it. But running at full speed consumed nearly a gallon of petrol an hour whilst making good no more than five miles on reasonably flat water. It had a nasty habit of spluttering when in a seaway and a terrible temper when you needed it most.

I always carried a battery of cold plugs to replace the hot ones, which were the cause of it refusing to start a second time. By the time I had completed a change of plugs, we would either be about to drift on to a sandbank, into the mud or, worse, into another boat. Once, being fast asleep at anchor in the Swale, a midnight gale caused my Bruce anchor to drag. The crew on the boat at anchor behind me were desperately trying to wake me up, shouting at the top of their voices to make themselves heard over the racket of the gale. They flashed their torches and banged their saucepans, which eventually woke me up from my deep slumbers. Popping my head out of the companionway, I saw the spectacle and realised the imminent danger of a horrible collision. I signalled to them that I had understood the problem and for a second considered what to do. Not having an anchor winch, there was no way that I would be able to haul in the anchor and drop it elsewhere without the help of my engine. I needed forward thrust to take the strain off the anchor chain so that I could haul in the anchor. Try as I might, it refused to start. The drift we were making in that terrible gale was unstoppable. I tried so hard to get the engine started that I flooded the plugs. New plugs. Tried again. No joy. The battery began to protest. I would try once more with a new set of cold plugs before I would have to give up, fend off and hope for the best. *Sally* was almost on top of the other boat when, miraculously, the engine fired up. Belching out huge oily clouds into the faces of the panic-stricken crew downwind from *Sally*, I moved forward very, very slowly into the tide and the furious gale.

It was always best to avoid having to use the engine. I had learned to cope without its assistance in many situations where other people would not think twice about using theirs. The surveyor I had engaged to look over the boat before I purchased her gave me great confidence from his glowing report, describing her as a seaworthy and sturdy little yacht, but reserved his judgement on the engine. My pride had been swollen and I had not been able to wait to take her on a first sail. My neighbour came with me to help me test her sea-keeping qualities on the River Blackwater. The wind was light, giving us the opportunity to test the various sails including the spinnaker. On our way back to West Mersea, where she had a half-drying mooring, I directed my neighbour to head for the power station at Bradwell, a large and unmistakable landmark, while I struggled on the little foredeck to hoist the last sail, the spinnaker, looking up rather than down or ahead. Suddenly, the boat lurched and came to an unexpected halt, nearly catapulting me over the side and putting all sail in a flap. It was late in the afternoon and the tide was running out. No matter what we did, my little *Sally* refused to budge. She heeled over more and more until the tide had run out, baring a sandbank. At the hands of its new owner, the beautiful little ship lay gasping on its side on unforgiving solid sand as hard as rock. As the tide returned, the wind came up and darkness replaced light. Once starting to float, she swung around, bumping up and down with the swell and hitting the bottom with every wave that passed. As she swung, I observed her rudder distancing itself from the boat, standing proudly like a truncated beacon marking an isolated sandbank. I did not then know that the keel had come away as well as the rudder. I stripped off and waded out, water neck high, to the protruding rudder stock. I managed to pull it free and gasped at all its beautiful broken bronze fittings. They were handmade and totally original, but they were kaput and forever unusable. Back on board we racked our brains as to what we could use for a jury rudder, but our imagination failed us. It was getting quite dark now. There was nothing for it but to try and sail back without one. Our course home and the wind were westerly, but I considered that sailing her back ought not to be impossible. The tide was coming in and if I could achieve seventy degrees off the wind we would not get home quickly, but we would get there. But try as we might, *Sally* would not cooperate. We were literally floundering. I could not understand why *Sally* would not respond to her large mainsail and began to wonder if we could get home to West Mersea using the flooding tide alone. Just as I was considering the worst result, a blue flashing light approached rapidly. Much to my consternation, the craft carrying the blue light seemed hell-bent on maintaining its course directly headed for *Sally*. I did not carry any lights and not having a torch on board either left me to consider my prayers. Having been alerted by some thoughtful passing fellow sailor, we were suddenly surprised to recognise that the blue light flashes belonged to a RIB of the RNLI. Despite its great speed of approach, the RIB came to a sudden stop within a few yards of *Sally*. Our immediate troubles were soon resolved and we were yawed back to West Mersea at breakneck speed. The following day she was hauled out and the missing keel observed. No wonder I could not get her to respond to the mainsail. An acrimonious insurance claim followed, but by the time spring came the following year, I had satisfaction from both the insurance company and the surveyor, who admitted liability. Shortly after receiving their cheques, I had a phone call from the previous owner, a well-known local oyster man, with the news that my old keel had been found by a local fisherman, washed up. Did I still want it? I was overjoyed at the news. I now had both the money and the parts. I had the boat shipped home where I carried out meticulous restoration work, replacing the keelbolts, rudder and plank fastenings. She looked a beauty once again and, having completed the Yachtmaster course at the Sir John Cass School of Navigation in London during the winter, I now felt confident that I would not let *Sally* down again.

When she was re-launched in West Mersea, she promptly sank in the slings. All her planking had evidently dried out and had opened up the seams in her carvel construction. The yard did not think that she would 'take up' and that she would have to be re-caulked. All my beautiful paint work was destroyed once the old caulk had been scraped out by a local retired fisherman. It was a fair introduction to boating, where more time, money and effort is lost than joy gained. But I kept her for twenty-four years, sailing the East Coast, crossing the Thames Estuary dozens of times and the North Sea to Holland, France or Belgium. Once motoring back to England for a lack of wind, halfway across the North Sea, just after the shipping lanes, I was hit by a fierce gale from the west. The sea was still flat, enabling *Sally* to scoot across the water at tremendous speed. But it was not long before the waves began to build. Soon the waves developed a steep side to their fronts, then began to topple, leaving *Sally* to wallow close-hauled. I bore off and gained some momentum. It would be a long haul back if we did not hit anything. The waves became mountainous and *Sally* had great difficulty coming about, but at no time did I feel that she was not safe. But an old wooden boat does not retain its strength forever. Its fastenings start moving, the wood is working all the time, there is rot in various places, and the maintenance may not have been up to scratch. There is no forgiveness in nature; no respite from nature's forces, and any weakness in the ship can cause its demise. Perhaps the refit I gave her after the keel had dropped off was now paying dividends. The gale was relentless and we were well past our estimated time of arrival. The family were agonising, the Coastguard had been alerted, and watches posted along the Essex coast had been notified of our predicament. When my crew and I eventually arrived in West Mersea during the course of the following morning in the teeth of the gale, picking up the first available mooring buoy under sail, for no reliance could be placed on starting the engine, let alone using it, we had a tot of whiskey before zonking out in a deep and well-deserved sleep. We did not have a radio on board to tell the family we had arrived, so their agony was unnecessarily prolonged. However, thanks to the keen observations of a watch along the coast, the family had been telephoned to say that we had been spotted.

Sally became in need of a complete refit. In 1993, in her eighteenth year of my ownership, I entrusted her to the International Boatbuilding Training College in Lowestoft, where she underwent a five-year rebuild programme. Other than the hull itself, all parts were replaced, including the keel into which the ribs were fitted, the deck, the transom, the stem, the cabin top and all the iron work was replaced in bronze by Classic Marine in Woodbridge, Essex. The Stuart Turner engine was removed and a new one-cylinder Yanmar engine installed on new engine beds. After much deliberation, the College agreed to fit the propeller through the stern-post. At the end of the fourth year of the rebuild programme, the College rang me up to request I take *Sally* away as she no longer offered any work that fitted in with the curriculum. I protested that all the furniture inside, which they had removed, had yet to be remade, but the College was adamant. They sympathised with my predicament and helped me by making available in their yard a space, where the furniture inside could be re-instated. They recommended a College-trained ship-wright, who was out of work and whom I ended up employing an entire year to complete *Sally*'s restoration. The cost escalated out of all proportion. At the end of it, however, I felt very proud to own this beautiful little classic boat and sail her on the East coast. She might have been a little too small, with only sitting headroom, and whose domestic arrangements would have been judged maybe less than primitive by the fairer sex, but she gleamed and beamed antique beauty wherever she went, inviting many admiring comments.

The year before I took my retirement, I considered taking *Sally* down to Portugal and into the Mediterranean, but then shelved the idea as *Sally* was not really capable of making much headway in an oncoming sea, of which I would have plenty, sailing south into the prevailing winds, plus I would not be able to fit her with an automatic steering mechanism, considering that she was so ill balanced. When I retired I sailed her on my own around the top of Holland to Germany, but the miles to Germany turned out to be the most frustrating ever, with little progress into the light easterly winds and her constant hobby-horsing. I decided to sell her as soon as I got back home and replace her with a yacht truly capable of sailing the seas without the frustrations and maintenance that *Sally* demanded. On my return to Tollesbury Marina at the end of the season, I entrusted her to the local broker with a price tag that came nowhere near the amount of money I had sunk into her but that reflected a big premium on the price that boats of similar length might go for. In the meantime I scoured the internet and yachting magazines for the ideal boat. My new boat would have to be no more than thirty-eight feet in length so that I could handle her on my own across oceans. She required a nice deep, protective cockpit that I had become so used to in *Sally*, a lead encapsulated keel (i.e. no keelbolts), one mast and tiller steering. I went to see a Giles 38 in Lymington and was quite keen to buy her, but the owner could not make up his mind and it came to nothing. I had seen on the internet a Rival 38 for sale in Turkey, but dismissed the idea as preposterous as I could not speak any Turkish and did not like the idea that she might be languishing in foreign hands. Moreover, I would not be able to work on her in Turkey and prepare her for sailing back to England. The legal documentation to transfer ownership would be a nightmare. In any case, I said to myself, it was too far from home to make it a logistically viable proposition. But there was nothing else that met my criteria, and my curiosity grew. There was no harm in ringing the broker. He might even speak a little English. The following day, with considerable trepidation, I dialled the number in Marmaris. To my great delight the broker turned out to be English and keen to sell the yacht. The owner, he said, was French and lived in La Rochelle. The Frenchman had sailed the boat there the year before and had put her up for sale. I had all the available details sent to me via the web with lots of photos. They invited a lot of questions. Her name was *Luna Quest*, which I thought an appropriate name for exploring faraway horizons. I felt the boat could be just right and decided to fly to Dalaman in Turkey to view her. I liked the boat at first sight and admired the space she had inside. There was a cosy double quarter berth on the starboard side, a wide berth in the saloon on the same side, although the berth on the port side seemed a little narrow, but comfortable in a seaway. A sturdy table between the two was big enough to seat six people around comfortably. Forward of the saloon was an invitingly shaped little door that gave access to the forecastle where there were another two berths and lots of space for extra sails. All the upholstery was in soft brown leather that would prove extremely useful in rough weather. She had a functional little galley with a stainless steel worktop, a two-ringed gas cooker with an oven underneath and a top-loading fridge. The heads needed attention, as did the engine, which seemed to be leaking a lot of dirty black oil into the engine tray. The broker said that all Perkins diesel engines leaked as though that was part of the boat and justified the mess. There was an impressive teak full-sized chart table beautifully varnished with a navigation station over it on the starboard side and a switch panel with some twenty-five fuses. It all looked a little forbidding after *Sally*'s put-you-up table that could just sit one person and doubled up as a chart table when underway. Built in 1986/87 she was launched in 1990 but had been ashore for some seven years in La Rochelle after one trip to the Caribbean while the owner got on with his furniture-making business. The present owner, also from La Rochelle and a friend of the first owner, had owned the boat for two years when his wife fell ill. I was looking at a lightly used boat with all my criteria met and a reasonable price into the bargain. We made arrangements to buy her and, as luck would have it, *Sally* was sold in the same week in April, 2005.

Much to my surprise, I found the yachting community in Marmaris to be completely western European dominated. Not only were virtually all the yachts in the two marinas owned by Europeans, but also most of the businesses that supported the yachting fraternity in Marmaris were European controlled, mainly by Brits and Germans. It was essentially a local cottage industry, employing a vast army of locals who all seemed friendly and proud to be working for the Europeans. I employed a Brit to survey *Luna Quest*. He, like so many others there, had married a Turkish girl and had made his life out there. On his advice, supported by that of the broker, I employed another Brit to carry out all the major work listed in the surveyor's report. The surveyor himself had been a Rival owner and spoke highly of the Class.

The previous owner had not been able to care for *Luna Quest* as much as I would have liked. The sails and engine, although serviceable, were tired, the anchor winch had long ceased working properly, and some of the running rigging looked decidedly suspect. The hull showed blisters below the waterline, which the surveyor had reported as merely superficial, but which he later admitted required the removal of all the underwater paintwork. I took the opportunity to give *Luna Quest* a new, additional protective gel coat before she was repainted. A local electrical contractor, together with a steel welder, provided *Luna Quest* with a gantry over the cockpit for the purpose of mounting two solar panels, a fixed satellite phone aerial and other electronic equipment that had been mounted on the pushpit, such as the Navtex and the GPS. The wind generator was also mounted to the gantry. The steel welder had clearly done this work before. On the inside of his cigarette packet he designed the frame, which would allow all the wiring to the electronic equipment to run through the stainless steel. I also replaced the rusty twenty-five metres of eight-millimetre anchor chain with seventy-five metres of new ten-millimetre galvanised chain, the weight of which I knew would help bring the boat's waterline parallel to the water's plane. Many more jobs were carried out, but the season was drawing to a close and I did not want another season in Turkey fitting her out. I rang an old friend of mine to help me sail the boat from Marmaris to France where I could prepare her for the ARC (Atlantic Rally for Cruisers) the following year. I could not wait!

Marmaris Bay

Chapter 2

Sailing at last

With the new propeller fitted and *Luna Quest* freshly anti-fouled, my friend, Spencer, and I set off under engine from Netsel Marina in Marmaris on Tuesday 18th October at 1015hrs. I had been anxious to get away as soon as possible as the autumnal weather was likely to get more and more unpredictable as it neared winter time. I had estimated the trip to France or Spain to take about a month, which would take us close to December, but today was warm and the sun was out, accompanied by a gentle offshore breeze, filling our hearts with propitious expectations. No sooner had we cleared the marina than an inflatable dinghy came racing up astern. I thought I recognised it as the marina dinghy. As it neared I thought he came to bring me something I had forgotten or left on the jetty. He brought his dinghy smartly alongside and the two boats headed out side by side at five knots. Unexpectedly, he said that I owed the marina mooring fees. I protested, as I had settled my marina bill the afternoon before. I called the office on the VHF and reminded the lady on the other end that I had been in yesterday afternoon to pay any outstanding dues. Yes, she explained, but that was for the period ending yesterday and would I please pay for last night? I considered protesting that I had explained to her that I was setting off the following morning; but going down that route would mean returning to the marina, tying up again and waiting for my turn in the queue to argue my case in the office, probably without success. Our minds were focused on getting underway, and we had already freed our minds from any land-based thoughts. I agreed therefore to pay the sum demanded, £21. We searched our pockets for the money and, as

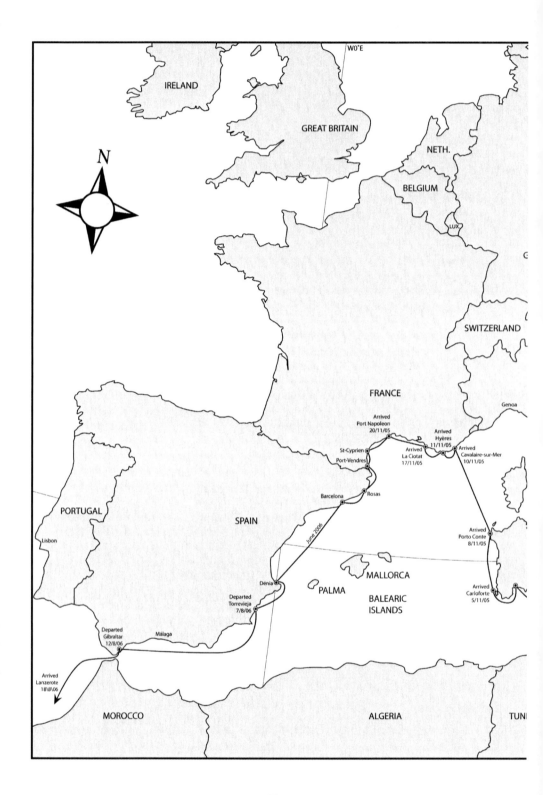

luck would have it, we just had enough notes and coins to satisfy the demand. We were now cashless, but were glad to be on our way and leaving Turkey.

The sun hotted up and, while the wind invited us to make sail, we decided to continue on the engine at least until we had left the bay of Marmaris. The new self-pitching propeller performed beautifully and I was glad to have changed the worn twenty-inch two-blader that had not been able to produce more than four knots at 1,800 revs. Now we were making five-and-a-half knots at the same revs. Later on we settled on 1,400 to give us a steady five knots. The Perkins 4108 diesel engine had been thoroughly tested and serviced, the injectors had been replaced and the injector fuel pump serviced off-site. In Turkey, it seemed, all services were instantly available and at reasonable cost. After lunch, when well out to sea, we stopped the engine and put *Luna Quest* on the starboard tack in a gentle north-westerly wind. Ideal for giving us time to settle in, finding our sea legs and getting adjusted for the days and nights ahead. Soon Rhodos appeared on our port bow while the sky began to overcast slowly with a little increase in the wind. A light rain now obscured the horizon. At six o'clock we had covered half of Rhodos' length and I felt a little disappointed at the apparent lack of progress made. I had expected to be well past Rhodos. Spencer offered to cook our first meal at sea, which pleased me greatly as I knew that he enjoyed cooking and that my cooking skills were a little rudimentary. We had provisioned and stored the boat together, so there would be no problem finding any of the foods. When he announced, after spending some considerable time in the galley, that he had decided to try one of the freeze-dried food packs instead of preparing fresh food, in deference to his sea legs, or lack of them, I had to suppress a measure of disappointment. Delicious aromatic vapours had been emanating from below, whetting my considerable appetite, but, oh boy, the result was unpalatable. Spencer and I tried manfully to eat our way through the grub, but it proved uneatable. Spencer gave up first and threw half his plate away. Another mouthful for me and I would have been sick. I chucked mine overboard as well. I now felt somewhat confident undertaking culinary duties when it was my turn.

We were enjoying a good Force Four, occasionally Force Five, as the night set in, accompanied by a slight drizzle. *Luna Quest* was sailing well, the Hydrovane seemed to keep her on course, and as we were sitting in the cockpit listening to the swish of the water rushing past, I became aware of a noise that I had heard before on my previous boat, but could not put my finger on it. I became concerned and looked for the cause. I soon traced it to the spinning propshaft, which because of the speed of the boat the propeller turned freely. I put the engine into gear, thinking it would solve the problem, but nothing happened and the shaft continued spinning. In the belief that a gearbox represents the one mechanical device that never goes wrong, I had not had it checked before we left. I now began to think how we were going to get into Valetta harbour in Malta in seven days' time if the engine could not be deployed, and whether the new cutlass bearing I had fitted in Marmaris would be worn out by the time we reached Valetta. I decided I would lash the shaft with a line to the various nuts and bolts that projected from the coupling and hoped that I would not forget to unlash it once we got to Valetta and wished to engage the engine.

The wind now increased to a steady Force Five on the quarter, the rain had gone and *Luna Quest* was dashing along at seven knots. It was getting on for midnight when one of us would have to bed down. Spencer insisted he take the first watch, so I crawled into my quarter berth and tried to sleep, but the excitement, the empty stomach and the commotion of the seesawing ship made sleep impossible. I reproached myself for not being in the cockpit and wasting the experience of a good night's sail. I lay there deliberating whether to rejoin Spencer in the cockpit or persist in finding sleep. The more I deliberated the more I stayed awake, so I got up and rejoined Spencer in the cockpit, admiring the night sky, the intermittent moon and what looked to me like half the Plough on the northern horizon. We were well clear of Rhodos now and into the South Aegean Sea proper. Little flickering lights on various small Greek islands confirmed our GPS fixes and gave us the reassurance that we were not the only ones in the world. Although it was not cold by any means, we both had our thermal underwear on to ward off the night chill. We were too excited to worry about being hungry or to feel sleepy, but by about 0400hrs Spencer tried his luck to catch some. He used the big quarter berth to leeward, but sleep would not come and he was up again at daybreak. It was then that I discovered masses of water slopping around in the heads' basin. The loo roll had been soaked, as had all our medical equipment in the locker behind. The cause was soon found, however. When on the port tack, the heel of *Luna Quest* would put the basin below the waterline, resulting in the sea coming up the waste pipe rather than any waste water going out of it. Luckily the waste pipe had a stopcock, which once turned off cured the problem. The loo roll went over the side and the medical equipment that could be saved we dried as best we could. It was something we would have to remember every time we sailed on the port tack. The second day promised to be a repeat of the first: a lovely bright start to the day with a little cumulus in the sky foretelling perhaps of a little rain later. The Force Five wind held and the sea motion was moderate. I set about investigating the gearbox cables in case these failed to give effect to the gear lever commands. There was nothing obviously at fault and the next thing to test would be the operation of the gearbox itself. We decided, however, not to test the gearbox because it would have meant running the engine and, if found to be at fault, would mean its dismantlement at sea, a prospect I did not look forward to. We decided therefore to leave it for the time being and consider matters again on a still day.

We were now approaching the north side of Crete and hoped to pass it before the end of the night, which would be our second at sea. In the afternoon the wind had abated to a Force Four and now reduced still further as day gave way to night, a process that does not last long. In less than an hour darkness reigned. Not having had a wink's sleep the first night, or any during the day, by the time evening had come it was almost masochistically pleasurable to feel the extreme lack of sleep. We could now nod off at will and at any time. The evening meal, however, had yet to be made, and it was my turn. Would I be able to do any better than Spencer? I was determined to give it my best shot. Mentally, I went through our provisions, selecting the fresh foods for our evening dinner. When the time for cooking had come I was glad to rise to the challenge and peeled away. I served boiled potatoes, fried sausages, onions and par-boiled peas, Spencer's favourite vegetable, with gravy and a mixed salad. I was quite pleased with myself and, helped by our feelings of great hunger, we devoured the food in no time. After Spencer had finished clearing up he put his head down whilst I in the cockpit alternated between fighting being near comatose and admiring God's world. *Luna Quest* forged on, unfed, un-energized and without complaint. I was mightily impressed how *Luna Quest* so relentlessly converted the wind power into throwing aside the waves, ploughing on regardless. Spencer surfaced at midnight to take over the watch. He had had four hours of undisturbed sleep and felt re-energized. He entered a new world when he came into the cockpit to take the watch.

We were now approaching the west end of Crete, where we would have to negotiate a narrow gap between several small islands before entering the Ionian Sea. It was agreed that the two of us would be on watch when going through the narrow Stene Kithiron gap as we expected that we might encounter some commercial traffic. I turned in and hoped Spencer would not forget to wake me when the gap got close, but there was no need, for excitement had me up before dawn. Rocks had appeared out of the sea to the left and the right, making us feel a little uncomfortable. Accurate navigation was essential. We both kept a sharp lookout. Our consternation could not have been greater when a huge tanker surprised us on a reciprocal course, passing between the rocks at what looked like some fifteen knots. It was the first ship we had sighted and we looked at the colossus in full admiration. Spencer offered to make breakfast, which was a generous gesture as the sea motion had become unpredictable now that we were in the Ionian Sea. A sudden lurch caused masses of muesli to shoot from a bowl he was preparing into the narrow door rails at the back of the cooker. It was my turn to do the clearing up. It was then that I discovered that the cooker surround was giving way. The screws in the timber proved too short. Spencer helped me remove it. No damage appeared to have been sustained, so we cleaned and refitted it with longer screws, which luckily I carried in my toolkit. The wind held steady all morning, perhaps a little bit too light for our liking from time to time, but progress continued to be made.

Just after midday the wind fell away to a very light breeze from the east. It seemed to present an ideal opportunity before lunch to experiment with the spinnaker boom and use it as a whisker pole for setting the genny opposite the main sail. I had not checked how to use it or how to operate its fittings before we left Marmaris. I found all fittings seized solid with corrosion and salt deposits. I did not think I could do the job on my own and asked Spencer to help. He had not been on deck since our departure and I felt a little hesitant asking him as I had the impression that he did not really want to venture on deck whilst at sea. However, the sea was slight and he readily agreed. The slight sea state was unlikely to produce a sudden rogue wave, chucking us over the side or any of the fittings or tools. Spencer put on a lifejacket, attached his lifeline to the jackstays, and clambered gingerly on deck, holding on to the handrails on the coachroof as he moved forward. There was noticeable relief in his eyes when he made it to the mast. Dislodging the seized fittings required the use of a hammer, but there was not enough swing room. I cursed myself under my breath for not having checked the spars sufficiently before we set off. While Spencer held the boom firm as best he could, I set about wiggling it, hammering it where I could, spraying it and twisting it. There was no movement; but we persisted and eventually, after some fifteen minutes, a little movement became noticeable. Soon we had it working, but there were two, one either end. The second one did not seem as bad. We were now ready to try the boom itself, which had two telescopic extensions, one within the other, held in place by two sprung plastic buttons either side of the tubular housing, which when depressed allowed you to pull out one or two extensions from the front of the boom. We were very relieved to find the extensions came out effortlessly, but it was no mean feat to attach the end of the extended boom to the clew of the genny with the other end of the boom attached to a fitting on the forward end of the mast, where that fitting was mounted on a track so that it could slide up and down. Spencer had gone back to the cockpit to manage the winches while I battled to catch the sheet leading to the clew of the flapping sail so as to hook the forward end of the boom on to it. Holding the forward end of the boom as steady as I could while trying to catch the sheet was a dangerous job with the wind trying to lift me off the deck every time a puff filled the large sail. I managed it after a good few attempts, but felt thoroughly beaten. I condemned the system as too dangerous in a seaway or if there was a bit of puff, and decided not to use it again other than in very light weather conditions. The exertions had sapped all my strength and I was mightily pleased to be back in the safety of the cockpit, where I recovered my energies. Some weeks later, on the advice of a fellow yachtsman, we found that the boom could be unhooked from the mast to facilitate hooking the other end of it to the clew of the sail or better still, he advised, to the sheet leading to the clew. He said that the boom would travel forward of its own accord in any case. I felt very silly having to be pointed out how to boom out the sail, because with hindsight it seemed such a simple thing to do. On *Sally* I had a different system that worked very well but was no safer.

For a time it looked as though the genny would do some work, but it did not seem to like being set square to the ship's centre line and refused to fill properly. I noticed a rather ominous curve in the extended boom and wondered about its strength. Was it meant to be doing this? Suddenly, there was a dull bang and a shaking of the mast. The boom's two telescopic extensions had collapsed and were back in their housing with the genny flapping uncontrollably in the swell. Having only recovered a little from my physical exertions, I could not see myself doing it all over again. I went on deck to inspect the plastic buttons. They were worn down and, under pressure, allowed the extensions to collapse. We decided to give up on our experiment, roll the genny and sail *Luna Quest* before the wind using just the main sail, hauling it tight by the preventer to stop the sail from banging about in the cross swell. We were fairly exhausted from these operations and had difficulty finding new energy to make a late lunch. The time was coming up to four o'clock in the afternoon.

After the light easterly wind had shown a little more life in the afternoon, it died by early evening, leaving the mainsail banging about the shrouds. We took it down and drifted like a cork on an awkward swell. We speculated on what the swell was trying to tell us but checking the forecast on the Weatherman gave us nothing untoward and we took the opportunity to take some rest. All night we drifted westwards in the silence of a moonlit sky and stars falling out of the firmament. However, frustration at the lack of progress got the better of us and at daybreak we put the engine on in search of wind further west. The engine sputtered into action and I was mightily relieved to find that the gearbox appeared to be working fine. On a smooth and glassy sea we motored at 1,400 revs, giving us five knots. Spencer loved driving the boat on the engine. It took him back to the days when he captained merchant vessels and he recounted some memorable stories. All day we motored and not once did the Perkins 4108 hesitate, a marvellous piece of 1950s' engineering. Late in the afternoon there was evidence of a light breeze and, despite Spencer's protests at silencing the engine, we put the genny up, which now held admirably in a smooth sea, giving us just over two knots. Gently and gradually the wind returned, but now from the south. Our speed improved. It was delightful sailing in the gentle breeze and on a smooth sea. Gradually, however, the swell returned, but now from west-south-west. We were still being driven by the southerly breeze along our course that sat on the thirty-sixth parallel. The wind seemed to want to veer to the south east and, when it did, it slowly increased in strength. By daybreak the wind had settled to around Force Five and a swell from the south-east had become quite pronounced, clashing with the lesser swell from the south-west. It made for an awkward sea.

Luna Quest cared not about the swell but sailed beautifully under full sail. Just as we were about to prepare breakfast, a squall appeared fine on the port bow and the wind increased to Force Six. I thought it wise to put in a reef in case the wind rose higher. Breakfast was delayed. We rolled some of the genny and put one reef in the mainsail. We were still making over seven knots of speed. Shortly after we had adjusted the Hydrovane, which we christened '*Sally*' after the name of my old boat, a rogue wave soaked the cockpit and it was time to put our oilies on in preparation for what looked like a bit of rough weather ahead. All morning and early afternoon the wind blew from the south-south-east in the Force Six range, clearing the skies in the afternoon. It gave us a wonderful bracing sail, despite the cross swell. The Weatherman forecast an increase in the wind to Force Seven / Eight on Sunday. We were already experiencing a tendency for the wind to reach Force Seven, and took in some more genny and main sail, but we still appeared over-canvassed. We dropped the mainsail and under a little bit more genny we powered west at over six knots. It was just as well we had taken the main sail down because the reefing lines appeared attached in the wrong places, making it impossible to set the sail properly with a second reef, let alone a third. Something else I had not checked and ought to have done before setting sail. We would have to put that right as soon as conditions allowed. Under genny alone, however, the Hydrovane would not maintain our westerly course, setting us more north than we liked. I thought about going through the Straits of Messina to the north-west of us, for which we had a chart. I suggested it to Spencer, but he was not for the idea, given the likelihood of heavy commercial traffic and insufficient sea-room. We therefore pressed on for Malta, although this wind would have been ideal to leave Malta to our port and make for Cagliari in Sardinia, our second scheduled port of call.

We were now over halfway across the Ionian Sea and thought that with a little bit of luck we could make Malta late the following afternoon. Our hopes were underpinned when at nightfall the wind remained as strong as it had been during the day. All night we pressed on under the genny alone, but just before dawn the wind dropped to Force Five and kept on dropping. At 0830hrs nearly all the wind suddenly left us and we were forced to put the engine on. The little wind there was came from hot Africa and enveloped us sultrily. A new swell from the south-west hardened by the minute, causing us a little discomfort punching straight into it. The wind, though, remained absent. I cannot deny my dislike for using the engine, but it purred so sweetly and so steadfastly, that I could not help admiring old fashioned British engineering for its reliability and durability. It leaked a little oil, but that was its only fault. I resolved to have that cured once *Luna Quest* was hauled out in France for the winter. The punching into the rising swell became harder and harder, causing tons of water to land on top of the boat, cascading off the coachroof and sweeping down the side-decks into the drain holes aft. In the saloon, I discovered streams of water down the inside of the cabin coamings and under the inspection hatch in the ceiling where the electric mast cables are gathered before branching off to the control panel at the chart table. Seeing water invading our private space made me feel vulnerable and small in the face of nature's ways. Without taking the ceiling down there was no way of knowing where the leaks originated. It was too rough to do anything about it. I put kitchen towels around the grab rails at the bottom of the coamings to hide the streams and soak them up. Curing it would have to wait until we got to Malta. All day we motored in a feckless wind, punching our way into the oncoming swell and hoping to make Malta the following day. In the afternoon the swell seemed to subside, giving us a chance to sort out the reefing lines. With the main sail down in its lazy bag and the reefing lines in a heap, we spent some hours trying to sort out which went where. Just as we were discussing how wrong the forecast had been, a light air from the north-east sprang up. We tried to use it, but if we wanted to make Malta tomorrow, there was no way this light air was going to get us there. So we put the engine back on again and motored until about four in the morning when the wind increased to Force Three from the east. It was now dead aft, but not strong enough to give us the confidence to set the genny opposite the mainsail and sail what sailors call 'goose-winged' because the swell was still strong and could throw us off course in an instant, potentially causing an involuntary jibe. When the wind increased to Force Four, however, we found the courage and the motivation, despite earlier misgivings, to goose-wing it. This time I did not use the boom extensions and attached the clew of the sail to the end of the boom without any trouble. The extensions remained neatly housed inside the boom. Now, with the two sails pulling, our speed improved considerably. Spencer was on the helm, watching keenly for any windshift on the electronic wind indicator. We had discussed the dangers of an involuntary jibe, but the swell was difficult to manage and, combined with a possible windshift, the risk of jibing was considerable. The Hydrovane could not be used in the awkward swell and was immobilised. Preventative steering was called for. Suddenly, there was the most almighty crash and the smell of burning as the mainsail crashed across. It broke the preventer, but otherwise there was no evidence of any obvious damage. The burning smell emanated from the cars and gave us a nasty taste in the mouth. Spencer was highly embarrassed and for a moment at a loss what to do now that the main sail was on the 'wrong side', the same side as the genny. He brought the boat back on course and, whilst recovering from the shock, the sail crashed across again, now back to where it had been before the first jibe. The fact that no equipment broke, other than the preventer, was a testimony of the boat's strength.

All day the wind seemed to want to blow harder, but Force Five was the best we got. We were approaching Valetta in Malta. The large-scale Admiralty chart indicated the presence of a red-and-white safe-water buoy with a white flash a mile off the harbour entrance. We were too far over to the north to see it with the naked eye and would need to jibe on to the port tack to sail towards it. Darkness, however, had set in and it was clear we would have to decide either to make landfall in darkness or heave to for the night and go in the following morning. Neither of us had gone into a harbour or marina in darkness before, and neither of us wanted this to be our first experience, but Valetta's friendly lights, although distant, beckoned and we decided to plot our way into the harbour with the help of our electronic chart. Hundreds of shore lights obscured the one light we were hoping to see, the flash light of the safe-water buoy. With his seafaring experience of making landfall at night in big ships, Spencer soon spotted the buoy and tried to point it out to me, but I could not see it, try as I might. We prepared to jibe. We had discussed in detail what each of us would be doing during the manoeuvre, me taking in the mainsail and letting it out again once the wind was dead aft and Spencer steering the boat slowly through the dead aft point. I had failed to tell him that he could expect some considerable pressure on the rudder once I started letting the sail out on the opposite tack. The manoeuvre commenced. We came to the dead point all right, but once past, a rogue wave lurched the boat over within a couple of seconds, causing the boat to tear up wind. The force on the rudder had been completely unexpected and the resulting weight of wind on the mainsail had been tremendous, the sheet tearing through my hands and taking off the skin. We now brought *Luna Quest* on the required course. The full impact of the easterly swell had significantly increased in size as the seabed shelved with our approach. Rising up and down the swell, the sight of all shore lights was suddenly cut off when in a trough and brought to life when on top. I wondered whether under these conditions we could put into the harbour at all, but we were now so close that heaving to further offshore did not seem an appealing alternative. Then I spotted the safe-water buoy and once we got close to it, we dropped all sail and started the engine. I went down below to the electronic chart plotter to give Spencer instructions on where to steer, jumping up and down the companionway like a grasshopper. There was quite a bit of commercial traffic coming in and out of Valletta harbour. One ship looked like a collection of lit Christmas trees, it had so many lights all around. Despite its size it was quite hard to identify and would have been completely blotted out against the thousands of dazzling shore lights if it had not borne away to starboard to show its full lit-up port side to us.

The excitement of making landfall in darkness had our hearts beating in our throats as we glided up and down the huge swell rushing towards the harbour entrance. We now saw the massive and forbidding spray against the harbour wall; entering looked decidedly dangerous. The electronic chart plotter, however, was dead accurate and before long we were in calmer waters inside the harbour. The harbour-master came shooting out in his motor boat to guide us to the marina. Spencer and I were completely exhausted and were grateful to be tied up where directed. After the very good meal that Spencer cooked, we took to our bunks and fell fast asleep. We had been at sea for seven days.

Chapter 3

Island hopping

Our few days in Malta were spent recovering from our seven-day non-stop sail from Turkey and investigating the leaks that had pestered us when punching into the waves. We removed the lining from inside the cabin and, with Spencer standing on the cabin top, spraying it with fresh water from the ship's hosepipe, I soon discovered where the water was coming in. Disused screw holes under the vent housing provided the sea with easy access to our private domain. The holes were soon stopped, curing the problem. On my previous boat, *Sally*, I had never been able to discover where the drips had come from. They always seemed to fall just where I slept at the lowest part of the sheerline. Only after a complete refit, which included a new teak deck laid on plywood, did the leaking stop. The leakage around *Luna Quest*'s mast was also cured.

After lunch on Thursday 27th October, 2005, we left the Manoel Isle Marina in Valetta under engine in what looked like excellent sailing weather. We laid a course on the starboard tack, sailing close-hauled in the gentle breeze. A large classic yacht overtook us on the engine, leaving us wondering why she was not sailing. She would have made a spectacular sight under full sail. There was a magnificent sunset, which I tried to capture on my disposable camera. The red sky promised another good day. It would have been a good day if we had not had cause to worry about the volt meters indicating that the batteries were not being charged. We spent many hours buried below deck trying to find the fault, but had to give up. I worried that if we were going to be underway to Sardinia for the next three or four days without battery power, we would in all likelihood be sailing without navigation lights and be without engine power to get into the marina. Sicily was nearby and we therefore decided to put in there. The nearest place was Marsala on the north-eastern side of the island, and we hoped to make landfall there the following day before darkness. Alas, a lack of wind slowed us down and had us wondering whether the engine might start. Luckily, the starting battery is separate from the 'domestic' batteries and had not been affected by the lack of power input. It started the engine immediately. We nevertheless could not make up for lost time and by the time darkness fell we fumbled our way forward towards Marsala with a handheld torch, which we shone all around from time to time, hoping that others out on the water would see us and recognise our plight. The sea had become like still water in a swimming pool through which we now glided with unobstructed speed.

The closer we came to the coast, the more little lights appeared spread around us. Spencer did not think it wise to attempt entering Marsala without an up-to-date large-scale paper chart of the port, but I was confident about our electronic chart plotter and persuaded him that as the sea was dead flat and the night as clear as a bell, we had more chance of achieving successful landfall here than when we put into Valetta. Ensconcing himself in the cockpit, he took charge of the helm, relying on me to give directions from the chart plotter in the saloon. Lobster pots and other gear began to appear in the water, but we managed to avoid them and kept heading for the harbour shown on our electronic chart. The coast looked uninviting without any distinctive lights that might indicate the location of Marsala. Could the plotter be wrong? There was not an alternative. Suddenly, a faint red light could be seen flashing, then a green. The electronic plotter had proved accurate and the harbour entrance lights became more and more prominent among the hundreds of lights on the low coastline that had hidden the harbour entrance from us for so long. We slipped into the marina and with our pre-agreed drill of making fast, we moored up just before midnight. What a relief to be securely tied up once again. We would have the batteries sorted out in the morning.

Perhaps he had not expected any yachts to arrive on a Friday night, or perhaps he had other plans for Saturday morning, but the harbour-master, who had cycled down the jetty to inspect the new arrival, barked at us curtly and incomprehensibly. He was a large man with a deep voice and rather too heavy for the bike that carried him. The only word I understood was 'office'. So we said OK but we were more interested in a nice warm shower and a leisurely breakfast before we were going to present ourselves to anyone or do any paperwork. He cycled off again and we sauntered down the jetty. It was a long jetty and cycling was definitely a recommended mode of transport. The marina seemed empty, deserted with a few boats here and there tied up. It looked more like an abandoned building yard with weeds growing here and there. We could not find anything that resembled a clubhouse, let alone washing facilities, but there were a couple of portacabins on the site, one of which had its door open. As soon as he spotted us wandering about he shouted at us. We went up to him and asked about the showers, which he reluctantly pointed at by waving his arms and bawling incomprehensible words at the same time. The other portacabin proved to house the washing facilities. It had a steel-mesh floor and a filthy steel basin hanging off a chipboard wall with a single tap suspended over it. There were three showers but only one would function, cold water only. We were not looking forward to staying here any longer than we had to. After our bracing shower we saw the harbour-master and were aghast at the demand of €38 per night, the most expensive we had come across anywhere, even in England. On the upside, however, he managed to understand that we were in need of an electrician. He bellowed at three men standing around a little fishing boat propped up in the yard. One of them, a little man, came over like a lamb trotting up to the bawling lion. This seemed like mafia country. A fisherman by background but electrician by trade, he gave the bawler to understand that he would be over to our boat shortly. Back on the boat, having breakfast, we were surprised by the little man. I did a lot of agitated talking in various languages, pointing to equipment and nurturing the hope that he would understand just a little of it, preferably the pertinent parts, but I might just as well have kept mum because without saying anything he located the fault within two minutes and said in broken Esperanto that he would have to take the alternator off as it did not seem to be charging. I was very surprised by that diagnosis as I had had the alternator 'serviced' at great expense in Marmaris. I did not argue and saw my beautifully renovated and re-painted alternator removed and taken away. He said he would be back on Monday morning.

Over the weekend we learned that Monday was a public holiday and that no services would be available until Tuesday. I began to wish we had never put into

Marsala and had carried on motoring to Sardinia as Spencer had wanted to do. But there was no way back and we just had to exercise patience. On Monday morning I thought I would just check with our bawler whether the chap was going to come today, but the bawler was not there and the replacement harbour-master did not seem to understand anything but his own language. Suppressing my frustration and employing a patient and kindly face, I laboured to explain our quandary. Thinking he was going to say something like 'Ah, today is a bank holiday,' or words to that effect, he said that the electrician would come at two o'clock. We did not know whether to believe him. Did he not know it was a bank holiday? When two o'clock came along, nobody showed up. I called again at the harbour-master's office. He telephoned the electrician. Yes, he would come directly. To my great surprise, he turned up armed with a new alternator of exactly the same make and size as the one he had taken off. He showed us the inside of the old one, which looked totally corroded and rotted and clearly un-serviced since it was first born. If the service engineer from Turkey had been present, I would have delivered a few words at him, but he was not and I kept the vilification to myself. To our delight the new alternator worked wonders, giving new life to the volt meters and the batteries. It was too late in the afternoon to set off and we would settle matters with the harbour-master in the morning. The following morning I went to see him. The bawler was back. I told him all was well again but that I was not prepared to pay for the extra night's stay as I had relied on the electrician coming to the boat in the morning as promised. We haggled and finally settled on €15 for Monday night. This was definitely mafia country.

On Tuesday morning, 1st November, we left at first daylight (0630hrs) in the hope of covering the 180 miles to Cagliari in Sardinia in two days and arriving there before nightfall. A lovely breeze from the south-east pushed us along under full sail at over six knots and as the sun rose we were looking forward to a glorious day's sail. The wind got up to Force Five and we began to speculate that we might arrive during the course of the following morning, but the wind dropped to a gentle breeze, falling away further in the late afternoon. Old Perki kept us going until eight in the evening, when a breeze appeared from the north-west. Although from the wrong direction, I calculated that an early starboard tack would give us sufficient room for a long port tack before making for Golfo di Cagliari, but the breeze failed again in the early morning hours and we were back on the engine. By late morning the wind returned, this time from the west, allowing us to hoist the sails once again. It was slow progress and we were too late to put into the harbour of Cagliari in daylight. Spencer and I had now gained more confidence in putting into harbours in the dark, and as its entrance was well lit, we had no trouble finding our way in and spotting where the yachts were moored. As on previous occasions, Spencer was positioned on the bow with a boat-hook and mooring line, ready to find a largish boat to hook on to and tie up alongside. We crossed the industrial part of the harbour at slow speed and made for the largest and nearest yacht we could find on the nearest jetty, but then discovered just aft of it a clear length of low unoccupied jetty, which looked more appealing. We tied up at 2015hrs and forgot the world around us. Soon, however, a young man came to our boat, calling for our attention. He spoke in excited Italian. Spencer went to see him but could not get rid of him. He came back into the saloon and said that the young man had demanded to speak to the captain, so I put my head out of the companionway and, digging deep into my language bin, extracted a word which I thought sounded Italian and might mean tomorrow. I said, "Domani," hoping it would not mean Sunday. I said it several times and did not care what it meant or what impact it would have on the young man. I was exhausted and could think of nothing else but rest. He must have got the message because he suddenly leapt into broken English, which I interpreted as, "OK, tomorrow you must go. This is private." That was the end of that.

I had hoped to put into a marina at the end of the harbour called Marina di San Elmo to collect a chart I had ordered from Imray, but had not been able to identify it in the dark. The following morning, having studied the pilot guide in detail, we were surprised to find that there were several marinas at the back of the harbour. Setting off under engine to find the marina of our choice we came upon a collection of jetties, which looked as though it might be Marina di San Elmo. As we were making our way towards it, a young man standing on the end of one of them waved at us, beckoning us in to come alongside. There were no signs or boards with words that corresponded with any of the names in the pilot guide. A little further along from where he was standing was a tug being sand-blasted, which did not look too inviting to moor too close to, but not knowing any better or being able to tell which jetty belonged to which marina, we followed the young man's instructions. He proved not to represent Marina di San Elmo but the marina next to it; he had leapt out on to the jetty, hoping to get our business. Since none of the marinas with a couple of jetties each were advertised, the young man clearly aimed to do well out of the confusion. Much to our surprise, there were several British yachts with live-aboard couples, who had come to this spot to over-winter. The young man had clearly hoped that we might join the live-aboards. We walked over to Marina di San Elmo, who could confirm that they had received an invoice with 'paid' stamped on it, but not the chart. They asked me why I had not come into their marina, a question that I had been expecting. I explained the tactics employed by the young man in the marina next door and looked out of the office window in the general direction of the jetty where *Luna Quest* was tied up. I then spied the same young man looking through binoculars at another yacht that seemed to be hesitating in its approach. At €15 a night it certainly represented a welcome saving on the fee charged by the Marsala bawly. The operator of Marina di San Elmo insisted that we move to their jetties, which did look much smarter and appeared to have better facilities, despite the sand-blasting of the tug not more than a hundred metres away. I thought that my chances of getting the chart would improve if I tied up in their marina, so I said I would if the charts had not turned up the following morning. The chart did not arrive, nor the day after, so Spencer and I decided to set off without the chart from Imray, relying instead on an old chart that was part of the *Luna Quest*'s historic inventory. They gave me a bill for €14.50 and made me promise to use their marina again next time we came to Cagliari.

Having abandoned all plans to sail direct to Port Napoleon in France because of the stormy forecasts for the Golfe du Lion area, where Port Napoleon is located, we decided to round the bottom of Sardinia westabouts and put into Carloforte in the Isle of Di San Pietro, a seemingly ideal place to sail from for the south coast of France. It was only a day's sail away and it would have been a lovely sail if the weather that prevailed to the east of the island had also prevailed to the west of the island. The day had started beautifully with a hot sun and a very gentle breeze from the north, but the breeze was too gentle to keep us on schedule, so we motored around the island and caught a new breeze on the other side, but it proved fickle and disappeared altogether by early evening. We carried on motoring northwards into a new light air, hoping to make San Pietro before dark. The light headwind now seemed to be gaining in strength and as darkness fell the swell and waves were trying to beat us back. The wind was dead on the nose and kept on increasing. I was loath to give up any motored distance made good by sailing out and tacking in so we increased the revs and relied on Perki to keep us going, but despite the higher revs our speed kept dropping while the waves began to wash over the boat. It was now blowing a good Force Five, occasionally Force Six, and it had begun to rain. Our progress had dropped to making two knots of speed. Spencer and I were in the cockpit, feeling frustrated and beaten. Suddenly, the boat veered way off course with the powerful hydraulic autopilot seemingly out of control. I switched it off while Spencer took the tiller. I tried to think what best to do next. I was grasping for clues. Then I noticed from the cockpit-mounted electronic speedometer that we were going backwards! I knew then that motoring had become futile and that the last twelve miles as the crow flies had to be sailed by tacking out to sea and back in again, making the total distance to be sailed some twenty-four miles at best. I hated the idea of having to go up on the pitching deck in the driving rain to hoist the sails, but it had to be done. It was going to be a horrible job. I hoisted the staysail first, which I thought I could leave up if the wind kept on increasing. I then hoisted the mainsail and gave it two reefs. Back in the cockpit, I let half the genny out. No sooner had I done so than *Luna Quest* sped off close-hauled at six knots, but to the west and away from where we wanted to go. *Luna Quest* was now stable and careered through the waves like a thoroughbred racing at Newmarket. Arrival would be after midnight, some four hours later. Dead on midnight we tacked for the last time and laid a course on the port tack for the channel of di San Pietro. It was 0215hrs when we tied up in the well-protected harbour, where there was no sign of any wind, rain or waves that had raged outside and had made our lives such a misery since rounding the bottom of Sardinia. Because there were no boats moving about the harbour we took our time tying up stern-to to a concrete quay, where a friendly neighbouring live-aboard Brit gave us a helping hand. The stretch from the south of Sardinia to Carloforte, which had looked so promising when we set off, counted as the worst sailing experience since leaving Marmaris.

We were now a week into November and the weather forecasts had taken on some deeply autumnal elements. The weather had become less friendly and highly changeable, with cold rain and high winds. The forecasts for Golfe du Lion were continuously given as Force Seven / Force Eight or more with rain.

Maybe the Mistral that blows fiercely from the north down the Rhone valley was holding sway over the area. It can blow for a week or longer, making everybody under its sway edgy and fed up. Our plan of making a dash for Port Napoleon looked more and more hazardous. We decided, therefore, to edge our way up the coast of Sardinia, maybe Corsica, and jump across to the south coast of France at the first available weather window. The forecasts for the west coasts of Sardinia and Corsica were reasonable but awful for the east coast of Spain and the south coast of France. Having received a reasonable forecast for our area, we left the charming and unspoilt Isle di San Pietro and headed north under power into a north-north-west Force Four. The waters outside the harbour are protected from the swell by two sister islands. As soon as were clear of Isle di San Pietro, we hoisted the sails and headed out to sea on the starboard tack. We planned not to go too far out to sea for fear of losing ground in case the wind shifted, and hogged the coast as much as possible. The first time we tacked on to the port bow we could lay a course parallel to the curve of the Sardinian coastline and made pleasing progress in the latter part of the afternoon, but in the evening the wind abated and later failed us so that Perki had to come on at just after ten in the evening. There was only a slight swell and under a star-spangled firmament we made excellent progress. With the engine pumping away, however, sleep proved impossible and I got up within minutes of crawling into my berth. Spencer loved driving the boat under power, so I left him on watch while I busied myself in the saloon. The wind returned in the early morning hours and on a flat sea we had some excellent sailing, but by breakfast time the wind failed us once more. It was strange to think that a few hundred miles away a storm was about to be unleashed in the Golfe du Lion to give the area where we were headed four days of atrocious weather. We decided to make for port and found a small marina called Porto Conte at the tip of Capo Caccia in Sardinia. There we would be well protected from any gales, the marina being almost entirely landlocked in a natural bay. The sun was out in a clear sky and on entering the bay we were suddenly overtaken by a stifling, still heat. There was no wind and no evidence of any autumn here. I stripped off my jumper and let the warm sun burn my shirt as I steered the boat through the very shallow, still and crystal clear waters towards the marina. We glided over a visible sea bed. Nearing the pontoon the waters were so shallow that I could imagine I was driving the boat like a car.

I was amazed we had not hit the bottom yet. There was a solitary wooden yacht moored, sporting the French tricolour, with some young people on the jetty not far from it, staring into a bucket of water. Perhaps they were the owners. In my best French I asked if there might be enough water further along the jetty to tie up, but from their answers in broken English it was clear that this was not the case. They turned out to be Spanish biologists, taking water and sealife samples, and had nothing to do with the French yacht, which looked as though it could have been there for some considerable time. We tied up astern of it. The jetty that led to the harbour-master's office was long and wide with lots of tiny craft either side. He confirmed our suspicion that there was nowhere with enough water to tie up further down and pointed to Porto Conte marina on the other side of the bay. We thanked him for his advice and pointed the boat across the glass-sheeted bay under a hot burning sun. We moored up near an old teak wooden motor cruiser from England. It looked very tired and unloved with its white hull paint peeling and rust showing through on the teak-wooden decks from the weeping stanchions. It probably had an aged owner, tired of maintaining the bright paint-work in a climate that has no respect for such labours. Its design looked pre-War, probably early 1930s judging by the shape, the fittings and the materials used. Its superstructure was all in solid teak, looking very sad. We were very tempted to go on board, walk her teak decks and take a closer look at the brass plaques and fittings, but our better judgement prevailed.

The marina did not offer the services of a diesel pump near the fuel jetty. Fuel had to be obtained from a roadside pump, not far from the marina, using canisters and carried to the boat. The canisters the yard had for this purpose were large, filthy, heavy and unwieldy. There was no way I would be able to carry them once filled. I searched the yard for a solution and found a rusty old trolley that I thought might do the trick. It had been made very gammily and had solid tyres on wheels that were not quite round. How I laboured getting the canisters on to it, and how I sweated, pulling the lot to the boat. I stopped on the way to regain my breath. The yard manager came over. Thank goodness, I thought, he has come to give me a hand… but no, after commenting on the advantages of the yard, he invited me to consider using his marina as a base for Mediterranean sailing. The fees were low, he said, and there were frequent flights to all over Europe. I said

I would think about it and at the same time cursed him under my breath. Once I got to the boat I was completely exhausted. Spencer helped me get the fuel cans onboard and into a position from which we could siphon the fuel off into the boat's diesel tank. With much spilling and cleaning using copious amounts of Fairy Liquid, we managed the task. The forecast on 8th November 2005 for Golfe du Lion was Force Seven to Force Twelve, but Force Five east of that area, just where we were. It was 180 miles across to Port Napoleon, or if we were forced to avoid Port Napoleon, about 160 miles to the Golfe de St Tropez. I rather fancied being in the St Tropez area. I had been there the year before with Marion, my wife, visiting the classic boat festival and celebrating the seventy-fifth anniversary of the dragon class with friends of ours, who had taken their dragon down to participate in the races. I thought about leaving the boat in St Maxime, opposite St Tropez, and I emailed them several times, enquiring after a berth. But there was no response. Perhaps another French marina in the area could offer us a berth if it really became impossible to enter the Golfe du Lion. We set off the following morning under a blue sky and a calm sea with a southerly Force Three on the stern, fully confident that we would find a marina on the south coast of France, but the sails of *Luna Quest* were soon too heavy to fill in the diminishing wind and flopped about in protest at the swell. Surprisingly, and contrary to the forecast, the little wind we did have dropped away to nothing, and it seemed weird that 200 miles west of us the sea was in great turmoil because of the storm force winds. We dropped the sails and motored north along the last bit of the Sardinian coast with the promontory that had marked the entrance to the Capo Caccia bay, staying in our sights until well into the afternoon. Corsica appeared on our starboard bow, which we were unlikely to see much more of as our course bore away from the island. It soon disappeared from sight and with it the lack of wind we had experienced. An easterly breeze sprang up in the late afternoon and, rather than rolling out our genny, we decided to try the lightweight sail that I had not had out of its bag yet. It proved to be a fairly new sail of similar dimensions to the roller genny, but very light. There were no hanks on it and it was clearly meant to be hoisted freely and act as a kind of cruising chute. We were delighted to see how beautifully it set and it was exactly what *Luna Quest* needed in light winds. I wished I had made use of it earlier. Our progress was swift with the new sail and we hardly noticed that the breeze freshened. By early evening it was blowing Force Four / Five and still freshening. We should have taken it down and used the roller genny, but I was reluctant to take the sail down as it was performing sterling speed. Lightning appeared in the west and we guessed that it must be the storm raging in the Golfe du Lion.

I had gone down below for a quick nap when all of a sudden there was an almighty bang with Spencer shouting several times, "Eric, your sail is in the water!" I quickly put some clothes on and dashed on deck, fearing that the sail might drag under the propeller, but Spencer had already pulled the beautiful sail out of the sea, where it lay in an ignominious and crumpled wet heap on the foredeck. The cause was obvious: the spinnaker halyard had parted just where it leaves the top of the mast. It was now blowing a Force Six and with the roller genny poled out without the extensions we continued our surge towards France. The lightning intensified and we speculated whether it was getting closer. Was there too much westing in our steering or was the storm easting? Sooner or later the storm would blow itself out and whilst the going was good we continued to fly before the strong wind. Suddenly the wind dropped and we had to contend again with flopping sails in a moderate swell. The storm centre must have decided to track elsewhere, unless the lack of wind just meant a lull in the storm. It was essential to maintain our speed before the storm decided to change its mind and come back to hit us. So, with all sails down we motored into the night at a reasonable speed direct for our destination. With daybreak the lightning disappeared in the west, but a row of ominous looking cumulonimbus clouds tracked east along our northern horizon. They made a spectacular sight with their anvil-shaped heads against a crystal clear blue sky beyond. We hoisted the mainsail, reefing it down to the last reef and rolled up the genny. We left the staysail bent on. We were prepared. With the engine off we slowly progressed north, watching the threatening clouds. The sun rose higher and stronger and other than the cumulonimbus ahead, the sky cleared. It then dispersed, leaving us on still water with no wind and heavily reefed sails.

The little swell we now had took on a different character; a bit of swell from the south-west and a bit of swell from the north-west. As we were debating the reasons for their sources, a new wind sprang up from the east, sending us at a good speed north. It quickly freshened to Force Five and under full sail we were making over seven knots on the wind. The day turned out to be just wonderful for making our passage to the south coast of France. The swell may have been a little confused, but the speed of *Luna Quest* and a stronger but easier swell from the east made us forget our earlier deliberations about the causes for the cross swell. Then, suddenly, we were stunned if not deafened by two massive explosions directly aft of *Luna Quest*. Having given vent to our subsequent expletives of surprise, we scoured the horizon, expecting to see the French Navy gunning us down. But there was nothing. We looked up into the sky, a beautifully clear light blue sky, and looked all around us, but could see nothing that might indicate where the explosions had come from. There were no smoke trails in the sky either, only a serene backdrop of sea and sky. We re-found our confidence and exchanged speculations as to what might have set off such huge explosions. Then another two such explosions occurred, and again we scoured the horizon and looked up. Were we in an active military zone? I rushed to the chart, but there was nothing to indicate a firing zone. The explosions had been too close for comfort and had frightened us. To regain our composure we agreed to put it down to the French Air Force having a day out over the sea with the authority to detonate four missiles over the first British ensign they could spot.

As the afternoon drew to a close, we became quite anxious to put into a French marina before nightfall, and as St Maxime had not responded, we decided to make for Cavalaire-sur-mer, the most western marina on the little chart of my electronic plotter. At 2015hrs in pitch dark we made fast to the visitors' pontoon. The place did not look very inviting, probably because November must have been well out of season. We would leave first thing in the morning for the next marina further west, which was Le Lavandou. It did not seem much better than the first, with hardly any facilities. Neither could accommodate us for the winter, all places having been taken. The Capitainerie recommended us to try Hyere as that was a big yachting centre. So we carried on under engine, motoring slowly into that marina by lunchtime, avoiding the many yachts that came out for an afternoon's racing. It looked big indeed and my hopes to secure a place for the winter rose.

Chapter 4

Solo to Port Napoleon

Twelfth November, a month after we flew into Turkey, Spencer went home, leaving me alone with *Luna Quest* tied up at the visitors' pontoon at Hyere. He chose his day of departure well: the weather had seriously deteriorated with thunder and lightning, low clouds, heavy winds and rain. *Luna Quest* tugged at her mooring lines in a Force Five, but the forecast was for much stronger winds from the east on Sunday and Monday. I put out extra fenders and extra mooring lines, closed all the windows, secured the main hatch and took out my laptop to start writing an account of our crossing. In the meantime I hoped to get a six-month winter berth allocated. On enquiry, the harbour-master told me that Hyere was full and that there was a twenty-year waiting list for twelve-metre yachts and a five-year one for yachts up to eight metres. He said that when the books for mooring allocations open on 1st December, the queues are long and early. I felt disappointed, but not desperate for I had a place reserved at Port Napoleon in the Golfe du Lion.

With Spencer gone I suddenly felt a palpable vacuum and an acute sense of loneliness. It made me apprehensive of the prospect of having to sail *Luna Quest* on my own to Port Napoleon, and I wondered if I would be able to manage it. Spencer had been such a good and solid mate, sharing all duties and watch keeping without a single grumble at any time. Having him on board had given me such a boost to my confidence. But had I not sailed *Sally* on my own for the last twenty-four years, a far more difficult and wayward boat? Had I not taken her successfully across the North Sea often enough, even as far as Germany and back? Was it because I lacked the moral support? I could probably get somebody to help me moor up in La Ciotat. I had tried to secure a temporary mooring in four places along the south coast of France while Spencer was with me, but his flight had been booked and crewing time for him had come to an end. I would have to get to Port Napoleon on my own.

It was now blowing a Force Seven / Force Eight from the east and the forecast was for more to come. The spray and weeds were blown horizontally across the breakwater, crashing all over *Luna Quest* moored on the lee side of it to the visitors' pontoon. The deck and cockpit were covered in seaweed blown across the breakwater. In a way I was comforted by the tumult around me, because it gave me an excuse to postpone leaving and adjust to the silence and solitude that Spencer's departure had created. The earliest day of departure might be Wednesday, nearly a week after our arrival, when the forecast gave some respite from the gales. I settled down to a quiet and relaxed few days and recovered my equanimity and some of my confidence. The weather forecasts, however, remained volatile and Wednesday's departure was ruled out by Monday's forecast. New gales were now due to lash us from the west, which would make my berth extremely uncomfortable and hazardous, as the wind would come across the marina and push *Luna Quest* squarely on to the pontoon with the breakwater directly behind. The protection, however, from the easterly gales had not prevented one of the six fenders, all lined up between the boat and the pontoon, from bursting. I bought two new fenders to replace the burst one in case another should give out. The forecast on Tuesday suggested that Friday might be a potential day to get away, so I took the opportunity to go to the laundrette and attend to other jobs. I also fixed the navigation lights that had shorted due to ingress of water. Later in the day the forecast changed with the prediction that Wednesday would now give a westerly Force Three to Force Four, increasing later to Force Seven and Force Eight. I called up a GRIB file from Meteo France to verify the forecast from Hamburg on the Weatherman. It corresponded with it and to make absolutely certain I also downloaded on my mobile phone a coastal forecast for the Hyere area. That confirmed both forecasts. As there was no other place in the marina where I might shelter from the forecast westerly gales on Thursday, Friday and Saturday, risking being smashed up on to the pontoon, I now prepared to set off the following morning.

As the wind had abated for the present, I would make my final decision in the morning.

I woke up to a clear sky and a gentle breeze from the west and speculated that the swell had probably gone down overnight and that if I went directly I should be able to make La Ciotat, thirty-five miles away to the west, under engine, despite the headwind, and if it looked as though I could not make it before night time I could always run into Bandol on the other side of Toulon. The die was cast. I rushed around, relieving *Luna Quest* of six of her eight mooring lines and four of her six fenders. I was at the Capitainerie at eight o'clock, the time it opened, paid my dues, bought a French stick of bread and sped back to *Luna Quest*. I untied the remaining two mooring lines and motored out of the harbour, making six knots in a southerly direction over the calm sheltered waters in the lee of the Hyere peninsula, a natural wall of low hills, woods and houses. After just over half an hour I had cleared the peninsula. Turning west through a narrow pass into the open sea and headwind, I noticed a slight swell from the west, probably as a result of the gale building in the Golfe du Lion. *Luna Quest* took the waves easily, dropping her speed to around five knots. I could see the next headland in the distance that marked the beginning of the Bay of La Ciotat. The wind had now risen to an occasional Force Four, dead ahead, but it had not affected the sea too much yet, so I carried on motoring, hoping this situation would not deteriorate, but the last half mile to the next headland was a struggle in the rising Force Four / Five headwind. The sea had become too rough to contemplate motoring any further with the speed dropping from three knots to just two knots. I hoisted the mainsail, leaving the engine running to keep *Luna Quest* headed into the wind, and put one reef in, just in case the wind was going to blow up earlier than predicted. I thought I would not bother rigging the Hydrovane for the short distance to my destination. I could always use the hydraulic autopilot, which for the moment kept *Luna Quest* nicely on the headwind course. Then I adjusted it slightly to give me a little wind fine on the starboard bow and unrolled the genny about two-thirds of the way. The sails caught the wind and with the engine out she sped off over the waves at over six knots close-hauled. That was at 1230hrs. With autopilot now off, I hand steered ready to tack before heading back for La Ciotat, but found that *Luna Quest* did not need my steering as she maintained course under sail alone. What a marvellous revelation! I put the tiller up into its rest position and decided to have some lunch. I admired her stability, her speed and steadfastness as she cut through the water without blinking an eyelid. I began to thoroughly enjoy having *Luna Quest* under sail and all to myself.

I now was mentally revising the operations for the next tack. It was the inner forestay that bothered me as it meant I could not just go about as I used to in *Sally*, whose foresail would automatically catch the wind on the other side once the tack was completed. Now I would have to roll up the genny before letting it out again on the other side. The boat would lose speed during the manoeuvre and might not have enough momentum to carry herself through the wind on to the other tack. When the time to tack came I worked as fast as I could, but by the time I had rolled up sufficient genny to pass the forestay, *Luna Quest* had lost her momentum and would not go past the dead point on to the other tack. In the days of the square riggers, going about was a major operation with the ship labouring 'in stays' for some considerable time. With a Bermudan rig, going about was an easy operation, provided the foredeck was clear. I started the engine to help her through the wind. I then unrolled the genny with ease to over two-thirds of its full area, giving her a seven-knot speed close-hauled on the port tack. Although the inner forestay was attached to a fitting on the foredeck, which was supposed to facilitate unhooking it to free the space on the foredeck, so that one could tack unhindered, I did not think I would be able to do that given the tension it was under, and besides I had nowhere to store the end of the stay. The layline for La Ciotat was at exactly ninety degrees to the boat's centreline and I calculated that I would get to La Ciotat in just over an hour and a half. What a joy it was to see *Luna Quest* plunging into the waves and riding over them with uncompromising determination. She steered herself beautifully with the tiller up amidships in its rest position. I could not have improved on her performance by steering by hand and marvelled at the way she held her course without any assistance. I was very pleased to be underway, and thought how I would have reproached myself if I had remained moored up to the visitors' pontoon in Hyere, waiting for the next gap in the gales and being battered about in the meantime. The sky remained bright and the sun shone uninterruptedly. I began to regret getting closer to La Ciotat, now clearly visible and growing in size and having to make landfall, so delightful was the experience of solo sailing. I took frequent bearings of different objects ashore just to make sure I was heading for the right place on the French coast. Less than half a mile off the marina, I rolled up the genny, put the engine on and headed *Luna Quest* into the wind to let the mainsail down. Under autopilot, I put the fenders out and prepared her mooring lines. I arrived at La Ciotat at 1530hrs, within half an hour of my original ETA.

During the night the wind increased to forty-five knots and its howling woke me up. My goodness, I would have been battered about in Hyere if I had stayed on that visitors' pontoon, given the fetch across the marina. It was four o'clock in the morning. I looked out of a porthole to witness the boats in the marina all heeling and shaking, pitching and plunging. The genny on a boat nearby had been unfurled by the weight of the wind and flogged violently. The boats that were moored next to *Luna Quest* threatened her safety in their dancing heaves and plunges on the swell that smashed into the harbour wall. As I was moored stern-to I went to check that the Hydrovane rudder blade was not in danger of being smashed into the concrete quay, but it seemed that the mooring chain at the bow was doing its job well and held my little home just clear of the splintering danger. The banging from the partially unwrapped flogging sail threatened the entire rigging of the boat. There was clearly nobody on board. I now saw that the sail was half torn and would before long shred itself into ribbons. The flogging, I thought, would put fantastic strain on its mooring points and on the harbour anchorage chain to which she, *Luna Quest*, and many other yachts were tethered by their bows. I wondered about the safety of that chain, given the combined force of all the yachts moored to it being battered downwind in the harbour. But all appeared secure and, having put a third stern line on the weather side, I turned in again. I slept fitfully in the din of the banging sail, the howling gale and the unpredictable motion of *Luna Quest* snatching and pulling at her mooring lines. At daylight the gale was still as furious. I stood in the companionway, admiring the cloudless sky and trying to blot out the din from the flogging sail. As I was wondering when the gale might subside, a young man came running along the quay. He spotted me and began to gesticulate in an agitated fashion, beckoning me to come with him. I rushed up the companionway and soon saw why the young man was in such a state of agitation. He was running to the boat with the flogging sail. It had broken its mooring from the harbour anchor chain and looked in a most precarious position. She was a lovely old classic wooden yacht of graceful lines called 'Mad Fal'. I estimated her length at forty-two feet. She would probably weigh eighteen tons. What the name meant I did not know, but it somehow seemed appropriate for the situation she was in. She was fifty degrees off her normal perpendicular position in relation to the harbour anchor chain and had crushed into a smaller plastic yacht on her lee side, which had as a result also broken her mooring at the bows. The boat to the lee of the plastic yacht was a little plastic day motorboat, which strained its anchor chain to the limit under the weight of the two yachts banging into it. What a spectacular mess! Venturing on to the classic yacht, moored stern-to the quay, with the young man we were nearly blown off in fifty-five knot gusts and, whilst teetering towards the bows, I noticed that the boat was open and used as a home, but there was no one on board. The light was on inside and I could clearly see the disarray of an ill-kept floating home. The young lad, who had beckoned me to come and help him save the boats from being wrecked, was very unlikely to be its owner and seemed more likely to be an employee of the harbour authority. The wind made too much noise to ask questions. A third person now joined us and together we tried to salvage the boats, starting with Mad Fal. The wind was so strong that we made no progress in our attempts to haul Mad Fal to its original position. Later in the day, when the wind subsided, the plastic boats were taken away, probably crumpled or at least badly damaged. Mad Fal was hauled back on her mooring. I was surprised to see that she had not sustained more visible damage than her white topside paintwork scuffed and her stern damaged by the concrete quay. The rigging still seemed intact, but her genny would have been a write-off.

A large area of high pressure over England was slowly pushing south with its isobars spreading to cover most of France. The forecast for Saturday was a north-easterly Force Four or Force Five, decreasing overnight. I made up my mind to go at daybreak, which would be at about 0645hrs. As the Capitainerie did not open until eight o'clock, I paid my dues in the afternoon and prepared for departure first thing in the morning. Other than having to get up in the middle of the night to adjust the passerelle to stop it from scraping on the quay, I slept extremely well, dreaming of the afternoon that I had spent walking around La Ciotat and enjoying the activities surrounding the 1720AD celebrations of warding off the soldiers from Marseille, who were said to have been carrying the plague. The alarm sprang to life at 0545hrs. Consulting the Meteo's coastal forecast on the mobile phone, the partially overcast sky apparently portended isolated showers. It confirmed the forecast from the night before and so, without further ado, I put on warm clothes under my oilies and cast off at 0715hrs. I had been wondering how to negotiate a group of rocky islands lying off the coast near the Marseille bay and had decided to navigate in between them to shortcut the distance to sail. There was an awkward cross swell, one from the east and one from the west, with the wind blowing gently offshore from the north-east, giving us insufficient sail power to cut through the swell. The sails were banging about and it did not take me long to decide to call on the services of Perki. The nearer I got to the island rocks, the more I began to worry that I had made an error of judgement and that I should have gone around them, but as I got quite close I discovered a large gap between the third and the fourth island rock, just as the chart had indicated. I then saw another yacht coming in the opposite direction, which reassured me. As soon as we were past the island's rocks and into the bay of Marseille, the swell disappeared and the wind became a steady Force Four from the north. Under full sail, *Luna Quest* made six-and-a-half knots wind abeam. I could see the end of the headland where the bay and entrance to Fos-sur-Mer began. I was making extraordinarily good time in the fresh breeze and got to the bay by midday. There were some eight ships at anchor waiting to go into Fos, a large industrial area. I had very carefully set out my courses to Port Napoleon on a local chart the night before, and it was of paramount importance to stick to them if I did not want to run into any sandbanks or mussel-beds, which seemed to stretch for miles on the western side of the bay, where the entrance to Port Napoleon was located. The channel to it seemed to be shared with the entrance to Port St Louis du Rhone and, after some anxious moments, I discovered the first of the channel buoys marking the dredged channel to Port Napoleon. I also noticed a set of high cranes near the entrance to Port St Louis du Rhone, which would be an easy point of reference for future approaches, not unlike the cranes at Felixstowe, which can be seen for miles from seaward, a useful aid to navigation, provided one does not fall into a false sense of navigational security as I had once done, sailing *Sally* into the Orwell and nearly risking the loss of my boat on the Cork sands off Harwich. The creek into Port Napoleon, with its mud banks and little old wooden boats and huts scattered along the shore, reminded me of the creeks on the east coast of England.

It was 20th November, arriving at my destination more than a month after Spencer and I had set off from Marmaris on a hot sunny day. The longest sea passage had been the seven-day sail to Malta. We had been to many places since, seen very few ships and only a couple of yachts. We had experienced every weather imaginable and when I woke up on the 21st, the yard and the yachts were covered in frost. The boat was hauled out and put in a cradle amongst the many yachts in the yard. It was time to go home.

PART 2

ACROSS THE ATLANTIC

Chapter 5

Early preparations

During the 2006 London Boat Show, in an exuberant and confident mood, I added my name to a list of participants for the 2006 ARC (Atlantic Rally for Cruisers) and paid the £500 entry fee. I did not have a crew lined up at that time but half thought that my son, Edward, might want to come, and his lifelong friend, Philip Hunter. Having paid the fee I felt committed to realising what I had always wanted to do, i.e. sailing across the Atlantic Ocean, if not around the world. There was a great deal to do to meet the requirements set by the organisers of the ARC. Port Napoleon was primarily a 'port à sec' with many yachting repair, spraying, rigging, engineering and sail-making facilities. Moreover, I had been very pleasantly surprised upon my arrival at Port Napoleon that the resident engineers were from Norwich and the resident electrician from Antwerp. They were to be my most trusted working contractors. The chief engineer had two sons. One ran the paint-spray shop and the other helped his father in the engineering shop. David Berry, the chief engineer, had said that he could stop the Perkins 4108 from leaking oil but that he could not guarantee that the leak would not come back again, as the engine had not been developed for the purpose of powering yachts, which could stand idle for long periods of time, causing the seals to dry out. He had given me a price to rectify the problem, and although the engine gave superb service I was fed up with having to dive underneath the engine every time it had run for a bit to mop up the oil from the engine tray and re-fill the engine with a replacement amount. It seemed to be a common problem with Perkins engines.

Whilst at the Boat Show I wandered into various engine stands, including Yanmar and Nanni, and lent a willing ear to the sales talk. I was impressed by the power output, the light weight, the small size and the fuel consumption of the modern diesel engines compared with the big, heavy Perkins 4108 that occupied virtually all the space available in the engine compartment of *Luna Quest*. The

Nanni dealer was just finishing his sales talk to a prospective customer when I overheard him say that the Nanni 4150 was a straight replacement for the Perkins 4108. While the customer walked away, I collared the salesman and had him tell me the benefits all over again. He offered me a large discount in the hope of securing a sale, and as the price seemed very reasonable, compared with the cost of rectifying my leak, I decided there and then that I would swap my Perki for a Nanni 4150. I paid my deposit and rang David the following morning to tell him the news. He had planned to start on my engine in the next few weeks and was a little baffled by the change of direction, but as he had not started, he would welcome the new engine and undertook to sell the Perkins if he could. Although the Nanni engines were made in France, the manufacturer insisted that I could not collect it in France. It had to be collected from the dealer in England and shipped to France for installation. In the depths of winter I drove my sixteen-year-old Volvo 740 to Norwich, where the dealers were, and then on to Port Napoleon with much else in the back of the car, including two brand new Brompton bikes, a new exhaust system and a small rubber single-person fold-up dinghy that I would carry as a standby in case my rubber tender got stolen. Marion had her reservations about my old banger laden down to its axles, but all went well and I got to Port Napoleon after two days' motoring, despite a snow storm that had closed many of the arterial roads in France.

A month later I had a phone call from David's son, telling me of the progress they were making with the engineering work, but advising me to ring the yard's offices. He would not say what it was about. I was stunned to find out that one of their cranes to be used for lifting out the old Perkins had failed whilst suspended over my boat and had suddenly run out, crashing its hook and weight on to the port deck, but thankfully narrowly missing David's son, who had been standing on that side of the deck to help guide the hook over the Perkins engine. I promptly booked a flight and flew down. I was aghast to see the damage done: the locker under the holed deck and over the loo had been demolished, the Harken deck track mangled and beyond repair, part of the teak toerail in need of replacement and the coachroof gouged out where the weight had fallen. I was even more aghast when I went to see the faulty crane, which had been parked well out of sight. The hook and weight must have weighed at least a ton, and I secretly marvelled at how *Luna Quest* had withstood the impact. The yard took full responsibility and invited David to make the necessary repairs. The mast had to be taken off and the boat, now denuded, was wheeled into one of the yard's huge hangars fit to house several Boeing 707s. I obtained a price from the paint shop to have the whole boat repainted once the repairs were done, because I considered they would never be able to hide the repair work from a keen eye and I did not want to be constantly reminded. It was a good decision because when she came out in the spring she looked new, complete with a new engine, new wiring, an electrical point for a towed generator, a Kadadyn watermaker in the damaged locker over the loo, now beautifully repaired, and a new cupboard over the diesel tank to house the Brompton bikes. The joiner had also made new dividers in the gun locker over the starboard berth. The wiring on the solar panels, fitted in Turkey, had been found to be faulty and this, too, was put right, together with a new regulator. 'Incidences of Cannes', the Sailmakers, made a beautifully cut sail that gave *Luna Quest* another lift-up, which would allow her to sail much closer to the wind. All these preparations had taken a great deal of time and effort, involving several trips down to Port Napoleon and requiring me to stay in a small yard cabin for several days each time to be available for meetings. At last in June she was ready for re-launch and I could not wait to get going!

Whilst the rectification works were going on, Edward, my son, had declared himself available for crewing across the Atlantic together with Philip, a long-standing friend of his. They had managed to stretch their holiday entitlement to a four-week period, but had not been able to secure an extra day, in case of severe delay. They were both very keen to have an Atlantic experience, but could not join me in Las Palmas, where the ARC started, earlier than the day before the start! This was against the rules of the ARC, but I argued my case and an exception was granted. Although Edward had had some sailing experience in *Sally*, and also in a Mirror dinghy in the Veerse Meer, in Holland, during the holidays, Philip had had very little. I was not too concerned about the lack of experience, although the rules stated that the crew had to be experienced and competent. I decided I would put them through an Ocean Survival Course to familiarise them with extreme circumstances. If, after the course, they decided that an Atlantic crossing was not going to be much fun, I would have to think again, but completion of the course had made them even keener on attempting to sail across the Atlantic and, being prepared for the worst, they could not wait to pit themselves against nature's forces!

Chapter 6

A coastal experience

Having bent on the sails, I paid my dues and left Port Napoleon the way I had come, on my own. My first port of call would be St Cyprien, across the bay of Fos-sur-mer, where Marion would join me for a trip down the Spanish coast. How lovely it was to be back on my boat and puttering out of the creek towards the open sea. A gentle breeze demanded the sails up and, with the engine off, it was sheer delight to feel at one again with nature out in the open. When darkness fell I noticed that the batteries were draining fast. I turned off the autopilot and every other electrical gadget other than the tricolour light and started the engine, but the alternator showed no charge on the volt manager, although the voltage level was over 13v. I became concerned that I might not have enough juice to start the engine on arrival of St Cyprien to negotiate the marina. I would have to call my electrician to seek his advice before Marion and I set sail down the coast of Spain. When I arrived, the engine started fine and having tied up I rang him. He was totally perplexed and showed great concern. He said he would drive round the following day to sort it. Marion would arrive in the afternoon. The following morning he duly arrived and inspected his wiring, scratched his head but could not understand the problem. He rang his equipment supplier for advice on his mobile, then confidently swapped over some wires and triumphantly declared that all should be well now. Delight all round when all proved well. Marion had arrived in the meantime and being in a celebratory mood we sat down to lunch in one of the boulevard restaurants.

Luna Quest had been allotted a slot opposite a yacht that looked very much like the famous *Joshua*, the steel boat that had once belonged to Bernard Moitessier. I could not help but admire the boat's lines and apparent strength. I went across the pontoon to take a closer look, called the owner, as the boat appeared open, but had no response. A trusting sort of owner, I thought. We had just locked up *Luna Quest* and were toddling down the pontoon to go into town, when a suspicious-looking, swarthy middle-aged Frenchman of large circumference, starkers but for his tight small black trunks and black hair longer than I had ever seen on any hippy or sailing bum, came tramping up the pontoon. He wore gold earrings down to his hips. Marion asked me anxiously if I had securely locked the boat, because in her view this chap typified the sort of vagabond that you would see among the sailing bums and rob you and your boat at the first opportunity. Coming back from our outing ashore and walking back up the pontoon, I spotted the 'vagabond' coming out of his boat. Bearing in mind Marion's warning, I could not see an easy way to avoid speaking to him as he now appeared to be on the very boat I had so admired. On getting closer, Marion stopped to engage him in conversation. Brave girl, I thought and carried on to *Luna Quest*, where I unpacked the shopping. Marion called me over from the 'vagabond's' boat to make Daniel's acquaintance. He spoke excellent English and started telling us that his boat was a sister ship to *Joshua*. Marion seemed to delight in talking to Daniel and it was not long before he invited us for drinks at six o'clock on his boat. He was Belgian and, far from being a vagabond, he was the most charming, knowledgeable and entertaining host, despite prancing about in his overly tight trunks all evening. Although he and his boat looked as though they might have been around the world five times, he told us that he had bought the boat locally some years ago and that he had not gone anywhere since the date of purchase, but that he would love to sail to the Balearics. One day, perhaps.

The lovely weather that had now set in augured well for our trip south. Our first port of call was Port Vendres, only some twenty miles away, a most charming little fishing village, where clearly new developments are resisted. Tied to the pontoon, I discovered that the heads would not pump out properly into the holding tank. It was soon apparent that the holding tank was chock-a-block, having been liberally used by the workmen in Port Napoleon whilst *Luna Quest* overwintered in her cradle. There was nothing for it but to discharge the lot into the pretty little harbour of Port Vendres. I opened all the cocks and put the marina hose into the vent pipe, whose good pressure forced the muck out. Bits of paper now floated into the harbour. Luckily, it was late in the day and there was not enough light for anyone to see. It gave me some anxious moments, though. Port Vendres laid on the most spectacular fireworks that same evening. There were many little boats in the harbour, admiring the display. The fine weather now accompanied us to Roses and then to Palamos, another charming fishing village. Unfortunately, there was very little wind, so that all of our travelling was done under power delivered by my new engine, which purred away happily. We had aimed to leave Palamos early in the morning to cover the forty miles or so to Port Balis, but found that we were not the only ones wishing to leave Palamos early. The local fishing fleet was in the process of assembling in full strength outside the harbour of Palamos and seemed bent on encircling us as we slowly motored out. Their big engines and powerful wash made us feel and look diminutive. We felt a little threatened and wanted to get out of their way. Then suddenly two very loud local sirens went off seemingly to call the last few recalcitrant workmen to duty. Some of the bigger boats now sped off at full power, followed by the smaller ones as though they had been waiting for the sirens' signal. It left us bobbing up and down in their wake, searching for our course to Barcelona, where we were due to meet some friends of ours. The marina in Barcelona was right in the town with the Rambla a stone's throw away, but it was hot and the stagnant water filthy and smelly. I was surprised to see several live-aboards at the pontoon. One of them, a Canadian, had his family with him and grandchildren. His family had converted much of his deck space to a nursery with green vegetables decorating the bulwarks. I suspected that this end of the marina was the cheaper end, where the water was allowed to carry all sorts of flotsam and jetsam, and no doubt a home to Barcelona's thriving rat community. I did not express that thought to Marion for fear of sparking off fits of anxiety. In the better part of the marina there were some seriously expensive yachts, mostly motor yachts. One was grandly named 'Queen M II', but the 'u' could not be lit at night and gave the boat the impression that it was still being completed. On my enquiry of the reason for it, the German captain said that all lighting on the boat was computer controlled and that there was nobody in Barcelona who could make the repair.

With our friends we set off for Sitges under engine, for the wind continued to refuse to put in an appearance. A little wind appeared in the latter part of our six-hour trip, giving our friends an opportunity to experience the idea of sailing. At Sitges I parked *Luna Quest* in a slot, as directed, where I could only enter bow-in first. Because it would have been awkward for the girls to climb over the pulpit in their evening attire I decided to turn the boat around to give them the use of the passerelle that connected the stern to the pontoon. Turning the boat around would require the help of our friends and I laid out a plan to effect the operation without the use of the engine. Unfortunately, just as we were implementing the plan, the wind got up, making it very difficult to pull the boat around, but we managed it in the end.

On 10th July Marion and I set off for Denia across a 170-mile stretch of sea that would take us well away from the land. The strong wind we had experienced in the harbour of Sitges now failed us, and apart from a brief hope of being able to sail in the evening, we motored twenty-eight hours. When Marion was on watch at daybreak she spotted a large school of dolphins playing about the bow of *Luna Quest*. They leaped clean out of the air, turning over as they plunged down, shooting across the bow to return all over again a minute later. We arrived at teatime and found ourselves in the most modern, cleanest and best kept marina so far. But time had us on our way again on the 13th of July to Alicante, a place I had always dreamed of as a place to retire to. It was only sixty miles further down the coast and I looked forward to savouring its romantic image. A good easterly Force Five gave Marion an excellent opportunity to experience *Luna Quest* under sail and with the genny poled out we made good progress. I wanted to adjust to whisker pole and asked Marion to take the helm. She was very nervous to be charged with such a task, but hesitatingly complied. Whilst I made my way forward, she lost the plot for a few seconds, sending *Luna Quest* into a near jibe. Having made the adjustment, *Luna Quest* increased her speed significantly. It was a fast sail and got us to Alicante an hour-and-a-half before our original ETA.

The imagined charm of Alicante was destroyed at first sight. A huge marina, catering for some 800 boats, blotted out the view of ancient Alicante from seaward whilst the boulevard flaunted thousands of fish and chip-eating holi-daymakers. But the grand old buildings and the width of the boulevard were still there and redolent of an age that corresponded with my notion of how Alicante might have been. It was a good place to celebrate Marion's birthday and a most enjoyable time was had sitting at a small table on a crowded terrace, elevated by steps from the pavement, watching the crowds surge backwards and forwards along the boulevard. The following day we set off for Torrevieja, a short distance that we would cover in the morning. Sailing gently in light winds we were able to discover the landmarks that had guided us in the past to a holiday house in Guardamar, such as the radio mast, and found ourselves quite excited by the sight of it. The marina in Torrevieja seemed chock-a-block without anybody guarding it. We motored slowly towards the end of it, hoping against hope of finding a slot to park. The end proved to be a narrow cul-de-sac from which we had some difficulty extricating ourselves. The manoeuvring must have woken the guard from his afternoon siesta, for he appeared tottering on the end of one of the jetties, waving his arms incomprehensibly. Whether it meant 'welcome' or 'we are full', or 'please go away' we could not tell as the language he shouted and the sign language he made were very foreign. We ignored him, kept looking around, found a slot and parked. The half high-rise flats to one side gave the marina good shelter but also the greatest stifling heat. The fair wind we had enjoyed coming down now took refuge behind the flats, leaving us and *Luna Quest* sweltering in a grubby marina. The marina operator reluctantly let us stay where we were. He said he would move the boat to another spot in due course. We handed over the keys and prepared to fly home.

Dolphins

Chapter 7

The last of the Mediterranean

Having been told by the weather experts at the ARC Forum in March that the best time to sail from Gibraltar to the Canaries was August, I now prepared to sail round to Gibraltar and then Las Palmas, where the ARC festivities would begin. I purchased charts, planned my route and asked Douglas, a retired airline captain friend of mine, to crew. Early August, Douglas and I flew down to Torrevieja and made the boat ready to set off. We would make one brief stop at Gibraltar. On Monday morning, 7th August, we completed our fresh food shopping and cast off at 1530hrs. Generally, I set off as early as possible in daylight to give myself and the crew as much time as possible to settle in and adjust to the boat before night time arrives, but Douglas was keen to get underway directly, so we headed out to sea in a gentle swell and a light wind. Progress was slow and I became aware of a cross swell, which gave an awkward motion to the brains. Douglas offered to do the cooking and, having had a few whiskeys, he cooked the two fat slices of pork chop freshly bought in the morning. By the time he was ready to serve up, he was not feeling too well, but tried to ignore it. We sat down to dinner in the saloon, with the evening drawing to a close, munching into our chops. Halfway through my chop I began to feel a little queasy. Whether it was the chop or the motion of the boat, I could not tell. I looked at Douglas, who looked decidedly poorly. He looked at me and whilst we were looking at each other's facial expressions, we were both overcome at the same time with sickness. Douglas managed to rush to the galley sink while I ran up the companionway, hoping to make it over the side. I did not quite make it, but lost most of it where I wanted to lose it. We recovered quickly and felt a lot better for it. The food went over the side. By the time I had cleared up it was bedtime. I took the first watch and thought I would let Douglas sleep as long as possible, expecting to catch up on my own sleep during the course of the following day if I had found myself unable to ward off insufficient nocturnal dozing. The gentle breeze failed at midnight and we motored for the next seven hours under autopilot, which was very soporific, allowing me to doze rather more than I should have.

At daybreak, still under engine, Douglas, refreshed after a full night's sleep in the forecabin, joined me in the cockpit. I took the opportunity to put my head down, but was up again at ten o'clock to a change in the motion of the boat. A northerly Force Three had sprung up, inviting us to make sail, but it failed after a couple of hours only to reappear in the early afternoon when I thought we would try the parasail. It was a big sail in a large black sail bag, which I had picked up in Port Napoleon. It had been specially made for *Luna Quest* in Hamburg at considerable cost, but I had considered it to be an important part of the rig, as much of our sailing across the Atlantic would be in the trade winds that blew from the east to the west. I was anxious to see it set before we left the Mediterranean in case it needed to be adjusted or recut and sent back to Hamburg. We brought it on deck through the companionway as the bulk was too great to pass through the foredeck hatch. Once on deck, and having opened the black bag, there seemed no end of sail coming out. We pulled and pulled, filling up the foredeck space. There was now so much volume of sail that it threatened to spill out into the sea under the life lines. Then there were some extremely long lines attached to it; we could not figure out what function they might have, and were completely tangled up in the sail. We struggled to unravel it, but gave up after some fifteen minutes as the task proved impossible. We reserved our judgement on the sail until we could safely lay it out on the land and re-consider our actions. We put it back in the bag, which now seemed larger than before, and forced it down the companionway back to the forecastle. Douglas had not been very enthusiastic at the idea of trying it out when I mentioned it and felt relieved that the exercise was over. I felt frustrated with this impossibly large sail that did not look as though I would ever be able to use it. I would not try it again until I knew how to handle it. That would have to be in Gibraltar, in the marina, safely tied up.

Wednesday was another day of fickle winds from the north-east, and the night another one without much wind but, helped from time to time by the excellence of my new engine, we were making reasonable progress. The Navtex (a computerised navigational warning instrument) on Thursday night at just after midnight warned of southerly gales in the morning for the area we were in. I had not experienced a gale in *Luna Quest* before and was loath to experience one so close to land. I decided to make all speed to Gibraltar, now only twenty-five miles away. Douglas was fast asleep in the forecabin with eye pads on, earplugs in and something pulled over his head. It was no good trying to warn him. I set the revs to 1,800 speeding at a near seven knots over a gentle sea towards Gibraltar. There was no evidence of the gale yet, but just as we were coming into Gibraltar, a couple of hours before daybreak, the gale struck suddenly with all its ferocity, but we were now inside the protective harbour wall, trying to find the entrance to Queensway Quay Marina. The marina was soon found with lights shining brightly and seemingly beckoning us. There were plenty of yachts' masts over the marina seawall but there did not seem to be an entrance. The commotion of the gale, the turning and the reversing in the confines of the small harbour to try and find the entrance to the marina, had Douglas up. Together, we peered into the darkness, willing the entrance to appear where marked in the pilot guide, but to no avail. We searched with torch lights, went around and around, searched again and again, but could not find the entrance in the dark. Then, suddenly, we realised why we had not been able to find it. The marina entrance was gated, locked and impenetrable to outside mariners. We motored past the marina and further along the main harbour wall. We spotted a small inlet on the opposite side that looked like a very protected little side harbour and which did not appear gated. We went in guardedly buffeted by the gale, hoping to get our heads down as quickly as possible until daylight when we would attempt Queensway again. Just as we had moored up to a tug that did not look as though it had moved for ten years, and snuggled down into our sleeping bags, we heard Spanish voices calling us. What could that be in this tucked-away little side harbour in the middle of the night? Someone in need? We poked our heads out of the companionway. No, there was nobody in need, but a powerful looking craft in soulless colours bearing words indicating the police were right alongside, with two men in uniform bawling at us that we could not stay there, that it was MOD property and out of bounds to us. They advised us to anchor out to sea. I thought they must be mad, and told them that anchoring would be unsafe in this gale, but they insisted that we could not stay there and kept hanging around until we had moved off.

Back in the main harbour I thought I would try and call the marina office. Perhaps there was somebody on duty. Much to our astonishment, there was somebody on duty who told us that Queensway Quay was shut for the night and that the other marina, Shepherd's Marina, was closed due to redevelopment work. He, too, advised us that we should moor out to sea until 0800 when Queensway Quay would open. I protested and questioned him closer on Shepherd's Marina. After much conversation the officer, or rather the night guard, said that we could try if we wanted, but that it was not operational and that there was no exit from it or access to it over land. We motored around to Shepherd's in the fierce gale, which was now howling in earnest and forcing *Luna Quest*'s bow downwind at some thirty per cent off her course. At last we found Shepherd's. It was open from the harbour and entry was easy. There were dozens of pontoons to choose from, mostly empty. It appeared a construction site rather than a marina, but we were soon tied up and we slept like daisies until... at about 0800 there was the most almighty, searing and deafening bang. What the hell was that? I got up to discover that we were moored right next to an MOD runway where pilots were practising flying their lethal and deafening jets. In between the take-offs and landings we called Queensway, asking for a berth, but they advised us that we could not come until the afternoon as the marina was full. All morning we suffered this dreadful, deafening noise every time a jet took off. When at last, in the early afternoon, we were allowed to come into Queensway, the marina seemed virtually empty. Considering that no craft would have set off in the gale we rather thought that we had not been told the truth, but why? We cursed Gibraltar for being so inhospitable.

I had hoped to see a little of Gibraltar and spend a few days recovering from our four-day trip, but Douglas said that there was nothing to see in Gibraltar, having flown there many times in a professional capacity, and that it would be a waste of time. Taking his word for it, we hauled out the parasail and found a long, clean jetty to lay out the sail and its sock. Once laid out, I immediately thought that the sail was far too long for *Luna Quest*'s mast length. Had I given the makers the wrong measurements? The German instructions on how to prepare it for hoisting were incomprehensible. With the help of another yachtsman, who had had the same experience, the instructions became clear. We folded the sail back in the bag in such a way that it could be hoisted directly from the bag through the foredeck hatch.

Chapter 8

Out into the Atlantic

On 12th August we cast off under a cloudless sky and in a slight haze, heading for the Straits of Gibraltar. Dolphins darted about everywhere; ships, tugs, pilot boats and other motorised craft littered the pale blue waters in the summer haze. Douglas was on the helm sailing under full sail with the wind on the quarter. I pointed out the risks of an involuntary jibe, but Douglas confidently replied that he had experience of these matters and that there was no need to worry. I therefore left him on the helm while going on the foredeck to put the whisker pole in so that we could back the genny and double the sail area. Suddenly, there was the most almighty jibe. The boat was reeling and careering off on the opposite tack. I grabbed the mast and steadied myself. Luckily, the winds were probably no more than fifteen knots. I lay the pole down and went back to the cockpit. I jibed the boat back on course and went back on the foredeck to bend on the whisker pole. Then, all of a sudden, we jibed again with me teetering on the foredeck and the boat careering off once again. Now angry, I jumped into the cockpit, took control and jibed back again. I could see that he had lost the plot.

The shipping lanes in the Straits take up quite a lot of the sea space available between Spain and Morocco. Small craft are confined to a narrow strip of sea either side. When the wind turned to blow from the west and into the Straits, we found ourselves tacking every twenty minutes without a reef. A lively Force Five funnelled between the Rock and Tangier, heeling *Luna Quest* smartly. I did not think the wind would hold and decided against reefing. Although *Luna Quest* sailed fast, the tacking made slow progress on the chart towards the open Atlantic. As soon as we cleared the coasts the wind fell away and the tide turned against us, running at about two-and-a-half knots. An awkward sea now met us and without the help of the engine we would have been set back towards Gibraltar and no doubt into the shipping lanes. Overfalls and tiderips held our navigational attention to a high degree of concentration until we were well clear of the land. We had now lost sight of the European coast while the Moroccan coast faded from the horizon. I absolutely loved being at last in the open ocean and was no longer concerned about any potential mishaps. *Luna Quest* sailed steadily under full sail and under the control of the Hydrovane. I left Douglas on watch at 2245hrs while I turned in. At 0130 Douglas called me up. There were numerous fishing lights and fishing boats all around and hand-steering was now called for. I disabled the Hydrovane and steered by hand, negotiating the fishing activities. I thought we would be soon out of this inconvenience, but every time I was about to go back to my sleeping bag, another few lights would turn up on the horizon. The fishing boats, well spread out with maybe a mile-and-a-half between them, clearly had some very long drift nets out with poor lights on the end of the nets. Suddenly, there was a scraping noise under the boat. *Luna Quest* had not lost much of her speed as a result. What on earth could that have been? I turned around just in time to see a driftnet line popping up astern. How it managed to escape the Hydrovane blade, which sticks into the water like a vertical knife, was a puzzle to me, unless there was insufficient tension on the line to stretch before *Luna Quest* was past. More vigilance was required and I stayed up to get us through the myriad of fishing lines, lights and boats. At one point, however, we must have sailed into the middle of some complicated drift line structure as a Moroccan fishing vessel, not far from us, made itself known and beckoned us to follow it. He adjusted his speed to the speed of *Luna Quest*, staying about a hundred yards in front, and guided us out of what he must have known for us to be an impossible position.

The trip down to Lanzarote should take us about a week and while the forecast was good for the next few days heading south, the Navtex now gave out gale warnings for the Mediterranean side of the Gibraltar area. We counted our blessings, enjoyed the sunshine and the gentle winds that helped us on our way. Douglas was beginning to enjoy himself, too. He would have a beer or two at lunchtime and a couple of single malts in the evening. The wind continued from the north, no more than Force Four with friendly white clouds on the horizon. We used the parasail when there was enough puff to fill it. The seas were gentle, smooth and inviting. We observed our watches and life became routine. I considered that I could easily be doing this on my own. The Hydrovane was utterly reliable, helped by the underwater profile of *Luna Quest*, and of sea traffic, there was none. On 18th August we were closing in on Lanzarote, where Douglas had flown to hundreds of times when he flew for Britannia Airways. He said he had spotted the capital, Arrecife, and suggested we change course and head for it, but I was not so certain. Given the GPS position and the landmarks on the coast, I thought it would be further south. He convinced me he was right, and I let him set the Hydrovane for where he thought Arrecife was and went down below to write up the log. I re-checked our position and did not trust our new course. I went up to check, to find that the town we were heading for had nothing like the entrance described in the pilot guide for Arrecife and what I was looking at could be nothing else but a town called Arrieta. Not only that, but I could see the bottom of the sea through the clear water and knew we were about to hit the ground! Despite his protestations I put the boat on a reciprocal course until I could no longer see the bottom and then made further southing. I made light of the incident and carried on as though nothing had happened, but realised that the end of my trip had been nigh. It had been a sixth sense that brought me up into the cockpit, just in time. Arrecife soon came into view and did not look inviting. I decided we would not go for the big smelly, noisy capital of Lanzarote, but for a smaller yacht harbour, a little further south called Puerto de Calero. At just after four o'clock on Friday, 18th August, we tied up in the sweltering afternoon. It had taken us six days. Douglas secured a flight back home for Tuesday morning and to while away the time we hired a car at the airport to tour the island on Sunday and on Monday.

I had hoped to sail around the islands with Marion and wanted the boat in a place where the next island hop would not be too challenging for her. The pilot suggested the south coast of Gran Canaria (Pasito Blanco) as a safe starting point and an easy place to sail from. Therefore, on 23rd August I sailed the boat on my own to Puerto Rubicon on the south coast of Lanzarote in readiness to hop across to Pasito Blanco, a hop of about 110 miles. It was a glorious day and a gentle breeze from the east had me in Puerto Rubicon in a couple of hours. I spotted a few ARC boats already there, flying their large ARC flag proudly from the forestay. It encouraged me to hoist mine and friends were soon made. On 28th August I cast off for Pasito Blanco. I did not want to arrive too early the following morning as I would probably need some help tying up on arrival and I did not think anybody would be about before eight o'clock. A fresh Force Five from the north-east under a cloudless sky met me as soon as we were out to sea, shortly after ten o'clock. I rigged up the whisker pole, setting the genny to the opposite tack; we were bowling along under full sail doing nearly eight knots. I considered that the wind might take off for the night and welcomed the exhilarating speed. Soon, however, the wind increased to Force Six. I became concerned that the increased speed would get me to my destination before sunrise! I took in the whisker pole, but we were still running too fast with most of the wind being caught in the main sail preventing the genny from giving the boat the balance required for the Hydrovane to do its job properly. It flapped about most of the time, so I rolled it up altogether and carried on under mainsail only, steering by hand. Thankfully, the wind moderated a little in the evening, as expected, enabling me to heave to with the tiller tied down and I prepared some dinner. At 2230 I unlashed the tiller and we were on our way again. The wind had now come back at Force Six, giving us a speed of seven knots without the genny. At this speed we would arrive at Pasito Blanco about five a.m. I had not reefed the boat in a biggish sea before on my own and was afraid of carrying out the manoeuvre without the help of the Hydrovane to keep the boat on course.

Of course, I should have just left the tiller to put a reef in and leave *Luna Quest* to luff up into the wind. The sail would shake a bit, but this might easy my task of putting a reef or two in, but it seemed I had been numbed into my position at the tiller, nailed down as it were, incapable of putting any such thoughts into action. I consoled myself with the hope that the wind would soon take off… I continued to concentrate on keeping *Luna Quest* on course and worrying about getting to the end of the island in the dark too early and overshooting Pasito Blanco. I thought I would stream some warps to slow her down. In between leaving the tiller I managed to extract from the bottom of the cockpit lockers the warps sufficiently quickly to stop *Luna Quest* from luffing out of control. I attached them to the mooring cleats aft on starboard and port sides and threw them overboard. They seemed to have effect, for *Luna Quest*'s speed now moderated to six knots. At about three a.m. we were off the airport of Gran Canaria where the wind accelerated to Force Seven. I now wished I had reefed the mainsail when I had the chance, and berated myself for being so incompetent and indecisive. How can you expect to sail this boat single-handed if you cannot even shorten sail in a Force Six? I asked myself, adding another accusatory expletive. I looked around and saw black white-capped monsters rolling down on to *Luna Quest*'s starboard quarter at terrifying speed. None, however, leaped on board. I was getting tired of hand steering and had become quite hungry. I thought I would heave to and take a rest, but no sooner had I turned up wind than *Luna Quest* headed straight for the glaring lights of the airport, which just appeared too close for comfort. I put the boat back on course away from the airport. A freighter's navigation lights appeared on the horizon's dark downwind from *Luna Quest*. As the lights became more prominent I judged that it was heading straight for me. It was going quite fast, despite heading straight into the wind. The angle it made in relation to my bow remained constant, which I knew meant we were on a collision course. I expected him to have seen me and change course, but the expectation grew more and more frustrated the nearer he came. I decided that he had not seen me or that he had decided not to see me, expecting me to move out of the way. I considered I could take evasive action at the last minute if required. All attention was now focused on the navigation lights as they approached rapidly. There was no change in the angle on the bow and collision seemed inevitable. I cursed the freighter and changed course. She glided past at a rapid rate of knots as though she were in a calm sea. I watched her as she chugged past me quite close at a fine angle to *Luna Quest*'s course. I then remembered my warps. Panic seized me as I realised that their lengths from the stern could potentially foul the big ship's propellers. If they were caught they would without a doubt drag *Luna Quest* under or at best break under the strain or rip the mooring cleats off the deck or at worst haul *Luna Quest* underneath the freighter, where she would be smashed up by the freighter's propellers. It was too late to start untying them without risking having my fingers taken off or losing an arm at the moment the spinning propellers would take hold of the warps. Some very anxious moments had taken full possession of my wits, obliterating all worries about the course we were steering, hunger or tiredness. I sat there, paralysed, expecting at any moment to be subjected to the most horrific accident and possibly death. The freighter would not even know she had just chewed up a thirty-eight feet yacht with crew and all her contents. The watch keeper might have noticed a slight tremor in the ship and would have put it down to hitting a sleeping whale. *Luna Quest* and her solitary crew would no longer exist. I stared at the warps that had twisted themselves into one massive solid hawser. I counted my last minutes. Then the freighter was past and nothing had happened. I thanked God for his mercy and promised to be a better seaman.

While I was calming down from the general paralysis, and steering the boat back on its course, sleep suddenly submerged me into the nirvana. Soon *Luna Quest* went out of control and wanted to race upwind upon the land. Fortunately, the change of her motion woke me up and again I had cause to berate myself. Sleep had now become a powerful enemy. It kept overtaking me and, each time it succeeded, *Luna Quest* would luff up towards the land, bent on self-destruction. The main sail would flap about violently and the ship's motion would change from ploughing to hobby-horsing with the crests of the waves flying horizontally across the deck. Whether sleep would be able to put all these noises and different experiences into a powerfully reassuring dream depended on how well I could fight off my enemy. Just as day was beginning to break and I had come to the end of my energies, the wind fell away quite suddenly. It fell away to nothing, leaving an awkward sea that threw me around like a cork. We had reached the bottom of the island at the same level as Pasito Blanco.

I took the mainsail down and drifted. Then I remembered the lines I had thrown overboard. I looked over the side and saw them hanging straight down. I started the laborious task of hauling them in, warped up in one solid mass. It weighed a ton and it took me about an hour to unravel them. I was exhausted. I debated whether I should have a quick kip and leave *Luna Quest* to bob up and down. It was too early in any case to get into Pasito Blanco. The seas were calming down and the sun was gaining strength. A light breeze returned. It would be a hot day. I hoisted the sails and forgot about a quick kip. The onset of a thin haze blanked out my view of the south coast of the island and made navigation a little awkward, but after a couple of hours the haze lifted and I could identify the harbour's entrance. I gingerly motored in, tying up at ten a.m. with the help of two harbour officers. Much to my overjoyed surprise the boat next to me was *Joshua*, the steel sloop that had once belonged to Bernard Moitessier, author of many sailing novels and national sailing hero of France. She was not much bigger than *Luna Quest*, perhaps a bit wider, but she looked a stronger design with graceful lines just like her sister ship we had seen in St Cyprien, but this one was actually called *Joshua* and this one, therefore, would be the very one that had been Bernard's home for over twenty years, and in which he had led the OSTAR in 1968, in which he had been knocked down half a dozen times and which had been badly damaged in a hurricane in Mexico. At that time I had not finished reading Bernard's last book, *Tamata et l'Alliance*, because if I had I would have known that after the hurricane he had given her away to a young couple. I knew Bernard himself had passed away a few years ago, so I very much hoped to meet the new owner of this illustrious vessel. There were plenty of rust patches on her deck and sides and one could see that maintenance work would be a near full-time job. I made sure there were plenty of fenders between my boat and *Joshua*, both tied with their sterns squarely to a high and unforgiving harbour wall and one line from the bows tied to a mooring buoy out in the harbour. There was nobody on board *Joshua* and I regretted that I might not meet the present owner before I flew home.

When Marion and I returned to Pasito Blanco in October, we were met in the marina by the HLR (Honorary Local Representative) of the Cruising Association of which I am a member and always fly its burgee. I had not expected any CA members in the Canaries, but during my absence the HLR had spotted my CA burgee from the rigging and had made it his daily task to check on the whereabouts of its skipper. He told Marion and me how impossible it would be to sail back to Las Palmas, the capital of the Canaries and the starting point for the 2006 ARC, as the winds would always be blowing from the north in between the islands and how they would always accelerate off the Las Palmas airport to Force Six / Force Seven, preventing any sail boat from tacking up. I told him of the thirty-five-knots of wind that I had experienced sailing down from the north and secretly worried that I would now not be able to get back to Las Palmas to join the ARC! He explained that it would be equally impossible to sail back via Tenerife, where the winds blew equally strongly from the same direction, adding that the sailing at Pasito Blanco was safe and enjoyable. Why did I not make Pasito Blanco my new home port? I now dismissed any plans of sailing around the islands with Marion in gentle breezes and any thoughts of sailing daytrips. The business of mooring up after a day's sail seemed too hazardous and strenuous, especially climbing the steel steps in the harbour wall that Marion would find quite impossible. All my thoughts suddenly focused on getting *Luna Quest* up the coast to the marina in Las Palmas, a distance roughly half of that from Puerto Rubicon to Pasito Blanco. If going up the coast meant waiting for a break in the weather, I would stay on board until that break arrived.

The following evening we met *Joshua*'s new owner, an Italian who ran a leather importing business in Las Palmas. He told us that his boat was not the boat that had belonged to Bernard, but a sister ship, named *Joshua* by the previous owner after the real *Joshua* had been damaged in the hurricane and given away. It was, he said, to all intents and purposes the same vessel. The Italian confirmed the HLR's weather woes, adding that he had tried to sail north twice with a crew of four and that he had failed after tacking all night. They had come back, completely exhausted. He now spent all of his leisure time maintaining his boat while dreaming of distant shores. I now seriously worried that I would not be able to get back to Las Palmas in time for the start of the 2006 ARC in a month's time. I had experienced the Force Seven on the way down and had not realised that it was like that every day and night of the week. I would have to set off from Pasito Blanco and re-join the ARC fleet in St Lucia! What a let down! I hoped for a break in the weather pattern.

It so happened that the forecast for the next few days expected a disturbance in the weather pattern. An area of low pressure was going to sweep down rather more southerly, upsetting the trade winds in the sea areas around the Canaries and bringing fresh westerlies, be it for only a short while. I thought I would make use of this disturbance; I suggested to Marion that we left overnight for Las Palmas, but Marion decided it would be safer by road and travelled back by coach and taxi in the late afternoon while I prepared to sail back during the night on my own. The forecast proved right and the wind dropped away early in the evening, having been pushed out of the way by the oncoming area of low pressure. I motored out of Pasito Blanco, hoping to find a little westerly wind round the headland, but found none and kept on motoring. It was dark by now and the swell was going down. The wind remained absent all night, leaving me to motor all the way to Las Palmas, where I arrived at ten a.m., just in time to have breakfast with Marion in her hotel.

Chapter 9

ARC 2006 preparations

The weeks leading up to the start of the ARC on the last Sunday in November were hectic. I had arranged for *Luna Quest* to be hauled out in the first week of November, scrubbed and newly antifouled. I flew down to make sure the work was carried out in accordance with my instructions and lived on *Luna Quest* in the yard for the week it took the yard to complete the work. Marion joined me a week later, but although *Luna Quest* was now back in the marina, she preferred to stay in a hotel quite close. I stayed on the boat, where I felt I ought to be. There were lots of little tasks to be completed, especially as they related to the safety gear. The ARC officials would inspect each of the 231 participants to verify strict adherence to the prescribed safety measures. Jerry the Rigger had offered a free survey of any part or all of the rigging. As *Luna Quest*'s rigging had not been subjected to a detailed survey when I acquired her in Turkey, I thought I would invite him to look over as much of the rigging as he would like, confident that, having sailed without mishap from Turkey, he would find *Luna Quest*'s rigging in top form. However, Jerry found that the shroud plates on the mast were showing signs of fatigue, with hairline cracks in the stainless steel, and advised me to have them replaced. An untrained eye would never have spotted them, but having been told where to look, I was quite shocked to see the fractures in the stainless steel plates. There was less than a week to go to the start and I had to make sure that they were replaced before departure. Jerry did not do that kind of work himself and I had to find a local rigger to carry out the recommendations. The only one rigger capable of such a job already had a queue of ARC customers all wanting his services to have some part of their rigging replaced before the start of the race on Sunday. I joined the queue and was given to understand that there might not be enough time to change the plates before Sunday. Disappointment engulfed me, but hope kept my spirits alive. I went to see him every day, no matter on what boat he worked, to ask when he could tackle my problem. He was clearly overworked, but my pestering helped as he now promised that *Luna Quest* was his next job. He would come first thing in the morning. Happy as a sand boy I returned to my ship and prepared what I could for the following morning. Of course, the morning passed and no rigger turned up. When I saw him working on yet another boat, he said he would come in the afternoon. This time he kept his promise and worked until late evening to mount new shroud plates. I was not particularly happy with the job because he had to adapt a different make of shroud plates to fit my mast. He said that "it would do the job". Replacement plates had not been available.

We attended lectures, went to ARC parties in the evening, and made many new friends. Such was the conviviality among the participants that good humour and reciprocal help got me conned out of €50 by a would-be British sailor, who claimed to be part of the crew on a yacht called 'Endeavour'. The only comfort I had was that I learned afterwards that I had not been the only one. At least another three ARC participants admitted to having been conned by the same trickster. One evening when ten of us had sat down to dinner along the boulevard in Las Palmas, we spotted the conman walking by, counting his spoils. Three of us gave pursuit, caught up with him, confronted him and thought we had the better of him. He was a big young man, well over six feet, taller and younger than any of us, but when asked when he was going to give us back our money he suddenly broke away and ran for his life. We returned to our dinner, recounting our experiences.

Marion and I had a massive amount of provisioning to do. We loved our little titanium Brompton bikes, which lived in a capacious locker over the diesel tank under the cockpit. They carried us around Las Palmas, a sprawling city with wide and narrow roads, full of shops, restaurants, shoppers, cars and belching lorries. We made several sorties a day to Cortez Inglese and other supermarkets. *Luna Quest* began to sit visibly lower in the water and I wondered if we had not over-provisioned, especially as the skipper, Paul, of the boat next to us, a Sigma 40, did everything in his power to contain the weight of his boat. Paul had taken on no fuel and no water supplies for his crew of four. They had put themselves in the racing division, as opposed to the cruising division that we were in, and were expecting to do well. The crew was going to have to make do with freeze dried food and water from the watermaker. Even the teabags had been rationed. On the Friday before departure, Marion and I took a delivery of fresh foods. They arrived in cardboard boxes, so loved by cockroaches and of which there are trillions in Las Palmas. One could hardly avoid stepping on them whether on any of the pontoons, the quays or pavements, especially after dark. We spread the produce out on the pontoon and washed each item by hand, ensuring any cockroach eggs were washed out. The boxes were disposed of.

Often in the evening there would be a gathering of new friends in some skipper's boat or on some pontoon and, having made several new friends, we did quite a bit of gathering in the fortnight before departure. When it was our turn to return the honours, I had a few cases of wine delivered in the afternoon of the day of the party. They had been put on the pontoon where *Luna Quest* was parked. I had to get the boxes into the boat and had found that the easiest method was carrying the boxes of six bottles each one by one backwards down the companionway into the boat. Marion at that time had been out with friends. The delivery had been later than expected and there had been less than half an hour to go before the first guests would turn up at six o'clock. I had been anxious to get at least a few bottles into the fridge, although I did realise that sailors are not too particular about the temperature of their drink. Carrying the last box backwards down the companionway, I missed the last step, lost my balance and fell over backwards into the edge of the chart table. Not wishing the bottles to spill any of their valuable contents, I concentrated on saving the bottles and let the box fall on my abdomen. A searing pain in the left back of my chest now prevented me from breathing for maybe ten to fifteen seconds, maybe longer. I could not get any movement in my chest for the pain and lay gasping with the box on top of me. When my breath started to come back, the pain told me that my ribs might be fractured. I scrambled back on my feet and cursory investigation confirmed that I had fractured two ribs in the fall. Breathing was difficult and painful. Nobody had witnessed my accident and if I could hide this stupid event from my friends and wife, who would no doubt insist that I saw a doctor, who in turn would probably advise abandonment of fulfilling my dream, the chances were that I would not have to disappoint the crew and put myself into lifelong depression. I knew that nothing could be done for fractured ribs and, provided they had not broken and pierced a lung, time would heal the fractures. The first test of effective concealment would be in twenty minutes' time when Marion would return with some of our friends. I determined to hide every trace of my agony. When the first guests came on board I put a welcoming smile on my face, got the bottles out of the fridge and pretended all was well. Nobody noticed. We had a grand party.

Edward's friend, Philip, arrived on the Friday before departure while Edward was expected at around one p.m. on Saturday. I had to make special arrangements with the ARC Office to prove that my crew were competent as they could not be interviewed by the ARC's inspectorate by the cut-off time. Soon after their arrival the boys settled in pretty quickly and started filming the scenes of festivity that accompanied the celebrations of the ARC 2006 departure. Marion's friend, Maggie, had flown in from Tenerife a day or two earlier to help with last minute provisioning arrangements. Donald and Christine, Philip's parents, had come to see their son off and check on the medical supplies that Donald as a GP had provided. We were not alone having guests on the pontoon. Many boats had families, weekend well-wishers and would-be crew hopefuls, asking each boat if there was a vacancy. Then there were the pontoon parties, for which the pontoons very evidently had not been designed. The weight of the people, together with the dozens of boxes of wine piled high, sank the pontoons below the water level, but the partying went on regardless. Some of the sailors would not be feeling too well on the day of the start.

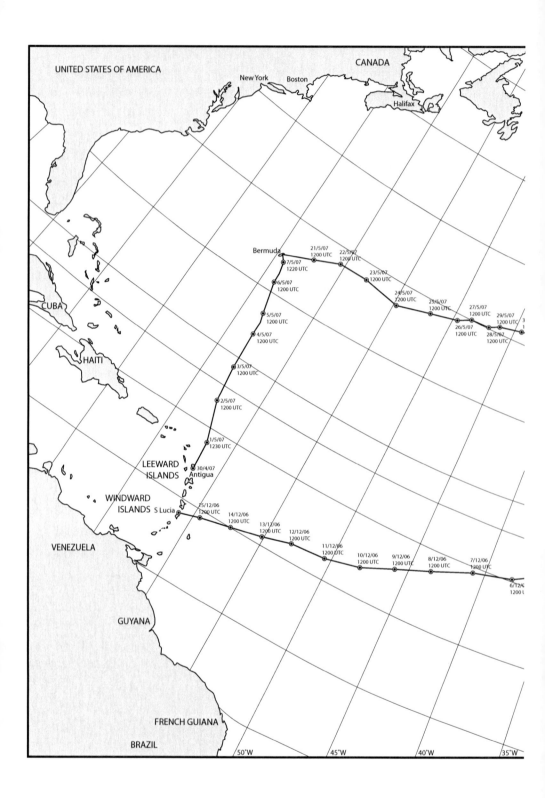

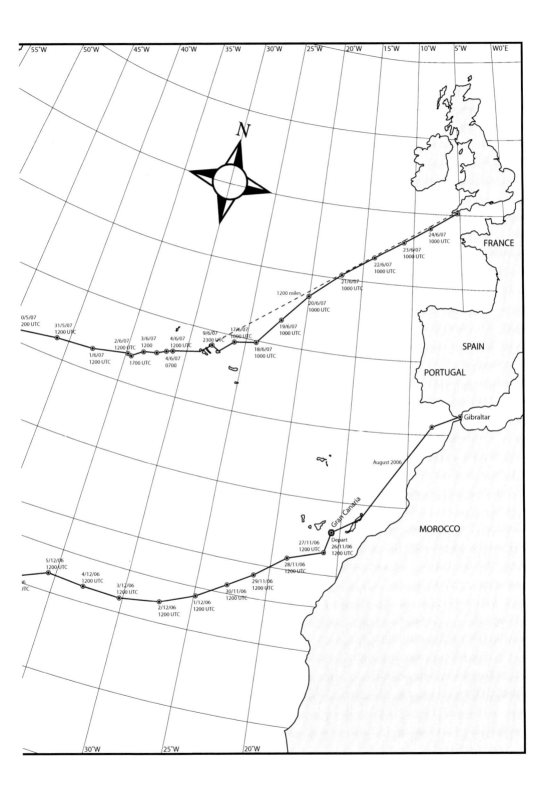

Chapter 10

The race across to St Lucia

Sunday morning brought a beautiful day with light northerlies. This was the day that I had dreamed of, daily on the train to and from work, in meetings, at dinner parties, driving the car and at any other time where complete focus on the job in hand had not been a full requirement. For over forty years I had fed that dream by reading dozens of sailing adventure novels, ranging from Chichester to Marcel Bardiaux, an intrepid French solo sailor who sailed his tiny home-built craft around the world from East to West via Cape Horn. Before I was due to retire, I had contemplated preparing my twenty-three-and-a-half feet *Sally*, built in 1935, to fulfil my dream, but an early retirement package enabled me to change my thoughts. *Luna Quest* had already been across the Atlantic with her first owner in 1992, a Frenchman, and it had been the ambition of the second French owner to do the same, but his wife had fallen seriously ill, which had put paid to his world-girdling plans. However, he owned another four boats in Ile de Ré, where he lived, and having *Luna Quest* in Turkey had become a long-distance liability. When I bought her in 2005, she had only been in the water five years of her first fifteen years of life. The first owner, after his transatlantic voyage, had laid her up in La Rochelle in the hope of sailing her again in ten years' time when his children would have grown up, but in the seventh year of lay-up he was persuaded to sell her to a friend, who sold her to me two years later. Now she was ready to cross the Atlantic again and fulfil the dream of her third owner.

The marina was full of hubbub and excitement. Bunting, flags and ensigns were flying off stays, shrouds and spars. The fine weather promised a propitious start to the race – I say 'race' because every skipper, whether in the race division or in the cruising division, would be seeking to get across to St Lucia before the next participant. The pontoons were cleared of boxes, tools, fold-up bikes and people, passerelles were brought in, engines were started and bunting brought down. At around ten a.m. the big class boats headed out, followed by the medium-sized ones and then the small class that we were in. One boat after another was applauded and waved at from the rocks and the breakwater that made for the narrow exit out of the marina. Hundreds of well-wishers thronged the harbour, shouting farewell messages and casting confetti towards the yachts. Once outside, the participants looked for the starting line marked by a large ferry and a post near the shore. We spotted Marion, Christine and Donald, although miniscule on the upper deck of the ferry, waving us goodbye. The yachts were milling about, trying their sails, getting their spinnakers ready and jockeying for the best position on the starting line. We were not planning to lose any points by being over the line too early, and hung back. There would be plenty of time to catch up over the next 2,800 miles to St Lucia. The gun went off and the big boats were over the line, hoisting their spinnakers as quickly as possible to gain the advantage as though they were racing on a sunny Sunday morning before lunch. Seeing them leap away south gave us all a thrill of racing tension and we awaited with bated breath the start of the medium-sized class.

The start of ARC 2006

At 1250hrs we were off in the bottom class, but we were not the smallest yacht at thirty-eight feet. Each boat had been given a number, ranked according to her size. We had been given 220 and the smallest boat carried 231. Those who had spinnakers hoisted them. I was hesitant. Then, seeing how we were falling back without it, I decided to join the pack and hoist the parasail. We had positioned it under the forehatch in readiness for it to be hoisted in its sock and snuffer. Once hoisted, it looked like a long snake with the collar of the snuffer as its head dangling at deck level. That needed to be hoisted now to reveal the parasail. As soon as the collar was lifted by its own halyard, the sock crumpled upwards, shortening the snake and the bit of the parasail thus bared caught the wind at once. The higher the collar was hoisted, the more sail was offered to the wind. Once at the top of the mast, the snake had disappeared and the parasail set beautifully. It proved just the right size for *Luna Quest*. I was very pleased to see it billowing out, setting so well and lifting *Luna Quest*'s speed considerably. Two-thirds up the sail, a vent spilled the excess winds and helped stabilize the sail. We now held our own in the very back of the fleet that counted some six boats only. I hoped I might be able to catch up with the 220 boats in front in due course. Number 231 turned back, a little classic from before the War, beautifully painted and varnished and probably around thirty feet. She did look a little pathetic, hobby-horsing over the large waves without making much progress in the light winds. I knew well the feelings of frustration that her skipper must have felt, having been overtaken by every other boat when I sailed *Sally*, especially when beating to windward. We noticed that some of the leading boats were heading more south-east than south and wondered whether they would be going via the Cape Verde islands or in search of more wind. We stuck to our southerly course and hoped to be making a little westing as soon as we had reached the bottom of Gran Canaria. Many of the leading yachts had already jibed to the starboard tack and were now definitely pursuing a south-south-westerly course.

Our plan was to carry our parasail during the day if conditions allowed and reef at night. When we reached the bottom of the island and put some westing into our course, we tried to jibe with the mainsail and parasail up as everybody else had done before us. It should not have been a problem, but having completed the manoeuvre successfully, we noticed that the parasail's halyard had got itself entangled and was rubbing on the stays on the wrong side of the boat. Not to do anything about it would have resulted in the halyard being chafed through in a matter of hours. As we could not untangle it, the parasail had to come down. That meant having to pull the collar down over the billowing sail as the vent would prevent the wind from being spilled round the edges of the sail if pulled away from the wind direction, the method used for conventional spinnakers. The two lads on the foredeck now experienced quite a bit of difficulty in bringing down the collar to snuff the sail, especially where the vent had been created. I would have been no help at all on the foredeck, given that my chest pains held me in the cockpit. The little wind there was seemed to be quite powerful in its will to fill the sail. In the end they managed it and the snake was restored, which we soon lowered, but I wondered how we would cope with it in a stronger wind. During the manoeuvre we lost hold of the collar's halyard, which is very long and whose ends are attached either side of the collar. Somehow or other we managed to lose the halyard under the boat in a great loop. Pulling one end pulled the other end down. Whatever we tried we could not retrieve it. The more we pulled, the less slack ensued. Darkness was setting in and as I suspected that the collar's halyard could somehow have entangled itself around the propeller, I dared not start the engine to head the boat into the wind to hoist the mainsail. We were just left to carry on under foresail only, which had difficulty filling itself in the light air. I considered changing to the light, unhanked genoa, that had given *Luna Quest* such a wonderful lift in the Mediterranean, but given that Edward and Philip were a little tired of the sail handling while they were trying to adjust to the motion of the sea, I thought it better to have a quiet night and let them have the sleep they needed. We set three-hour watches and turned in.

The entire fleet, including the five boats that had accompanied us in the rear, disappeared over the horizon. We were left bobbing up and down, feeling a little dejected and let down. However, the weather continued fair and the seas were kind. They helped us put in a good night's sleep and get used to the motion of the boat, but in the morning we were still bobbing up and down and not much further away from Maspalomas than we were last night, as evidenced by the strength of the powerful light of the Maspalomas lighthouse. Maybe we should do the sensible thing and return to the land, where my ribs would be given a full chance of recovery and the sail sorted out. I dismissed the thought as fast as it had entered my head. We would have to sort the problem out here and now and aim to get going as fast as possible. I investigated how I could best tackle our predicament. It seemed that there was nothing for it but to cut the collar's halyard off the lip attached to the collar. I unravelled the stitching, which I could see had been effected with great care and attention and German thoroughness. Once undone, it pulled free from under the boat. A sigh of great relief all round. I then spent an hour re-stitching it back as best I could and as strongly as I could, with waxed and virtually unbreakable twine that the sail maker in France had provided me with. By late morning the job was completed. As we were now a day behind the fleet, I rated our chances of catching up as very low. We sent the parasail up again and rolled up the genoa to give the parasail all the wind available. One tack was attached to the rolled-up genoa by way of a soft fitting that the parasail makers had provided, and the other tack attached to the end of the spinnaker boom by a large shackle, and hauled tight on the spinnaker sheet. The boom itself was pulled down by a line called the downhaul and attached to the forward mooring cleat. We decided not to hoist the mainsail and to let *Luna Quest* be powered by the parasail only. It was a grand sight to see all this sail silhouetted against the blue sky, firm in its purpose and steadfast in its duty. The wind was reasonably firm and nearly dead aft, just right to fly the sail. The Hydrovane had no difficulty keeping the ship dead on course. We could relax and enjoy the sunshine, the birdlife, the waves and nature's wonderful display of colours between sky and sea.

From time to time, however, some passing wave would roll under her at a slight angle from stern to stem, forcing *Luna Quest* to roll with it. The parasail as a result of the roll would want to collapse. We would have to jerk the lee sheet hard in to make the sail catch new wind. It was quite exhilarating for a while, trying to anticipate the next roll, but after a while it began to be a tiresome task. We would not have enough arms or energy to manage the sail in this fashion across the Atlantic. We would have to devise a system that would allow us to leave the parasail untouched, letting it do all the work while we occupied ourselves with the more important aspects of life, such as sunbathing, cooking and sleeping. Luckily, the wind began to blow more strongly, lessening the risk of sail collapse, but of course the seas began to offer higher waves, making the rolling worse and bringing back the risk of collapse, although it seemed that the parasail tended to hold better, but it still demanded our constant attention. Before long its demands for human effort outstripped our muscle or energy power. Something had to be done. I hit on the idea of rigging up the whisker pole on the opposite side to the boom and attaching the tack of the sail now tied to the rolled-up genoa to the whisker pole. It would allow the sail to catch the wind more evenly, and provided we could stabilise the boom and the pole, our chances of a set sail would surely improve. The weather sheet was now run through the whisker pole-end fitting and hauled back. The sail seemed to like the new configuration, but again every time she rolled the imminent collapse would result in both tacks of the sail sliding down the sheets at different speeds. The solution appeared obvious. If we could attach both tacks directly to the pole- and boom-end fittings without shackles, the sheets would no longer function as a slide but merely to stabilise the pole and the boom. Of course, it would be difficult to take the tacks out of the fittings in an emergency. But the winds were unlikely to whip up to over forty knots, the wind speed that the parasail maker had told me the sail was made to withstand. I had no concerns about the strength of the boat and secretly I hoped we would have some strong winds in the trade wind belt, when other participants were likely to either shorten sail or heave to. So I decided to go for it. Edward and Philip were balancing on the foredeck to carry out the task, Philip holding the boom first and then the pole while Edward attached the tacks of the sail. The boom and pole were securely fastened by their uphauls and downhauls and hauled back by the sheets. The result was marvellous. The sail stood proudly firm and seemed to withstand the threat of collapse. Every time it was on the verge of collapse as a result of some awkward wave, it redressed itself with a bang. I don't think we could have steered better than the Hydrovane or managed the sail better than the wind itself. We were romping along and our spirits rose considerably.

It stayed up all night without fail, occasionally threatening to collapse, but quickly filling again. Our speed increased to seven knots and it was only blowing a Force Four. *Luna Quest* definitely liked the rig and we liked her speed. She hummed. Seas were coming up behind her with little white caps, which all passed us by harmlessly. The deck was dry. When evening fell it was my turn to take the watch. I was alone in the cockpit, Philip and Edward having taken to their bunks, trying to sleep in our cradle craft on the high seas. At about 2130hrs

I became aware of being followed by a motor vessel that carried no navigation lights. It was probably a hundred metres away. I could not make out its size, but knew it was travelling faster than *Luna Quest* by the reduction in the dimness of its solitary internal light. The closer it came, the more concerned I became. Our tricolour light shone brightly and provided our follower with a clear and direct target. What were its intentions? Was he in trouble or did he want to ask us something? I felt a cold sweat creeping over my body as I realised that there might be more to it than just a social encounter. I would not be able to communicate with them in any case as they were unlikely to be fluent English speakers. I changed course. So did they and were gaining. I changed course again, now in the opposite direction. They did the same. The dim light became clearer and an outline of the vessel became more noticeable. What was going on did not seem to me an exercise of the right to free passage. I decided to switch my navigation lights off and start the engine to increase the boat's speed if that was at all possible. The boys came on deck demanding to know why I had put the engine on, disturbing their sleep. I pointed to the vessel behind us, told them the story and, as we were gazing at our pursuer, I noticed that we were slowly outrunning his speed. After about three-quarters of an hour's running on a different course at 2,000 revs we seemed to have lost our pursuer. The dim light had faded away. We felt a little safer. The engine was turned off. Peace had returned. Could they have been 'the boat people' that we had been warned against; people from Senegal that were trying to get to the European Union via the Canaries? Perhaps they were pirates. We had been told that all kinds of craft were being employed by the Africans to get across, loaded to the gunnels with emigrants desperate to start a new life. Maybe that was why the boat had not been able to increase its speed when we had increased ours; they had been going at full speed. If they had tried to make for the Canaries, they had clearly lost their way and if they had not been the boat people, they would have been up to no good.

The wind grew stronger throughout the following day until it was blowing twenty-five knots, where it seemed to stay. *Luna Quest* rolled a little more now and had started to vibrate to accompany the humming. Large waves came up her rear, passing at great speed, but leaving her deck dry. There was not a yacht or boat in sight. Somehow, I expected to see the tail end of the fleet on the horizon or something, but we were in the middle of our own little world with the horizon all around us. For the first time in my life I became acutely aware of our insignificance, and how vulnerable we humans are upon our oceans. On the fourth day out we spotted a yacht on the horizon in front of us. Perhaps it had a spot of trouble? Could it be an ARC competitor? It gave us a boost to our morale. Perhaps we were catching up; perhaps all the other participants had put a reef in and taken their spinnakers down! Our parasail was doing wonders. It never seemed to collapse any more. It liked being full of wind, which was now dead aft. It must have got bored with collapsing and filling. The weather remained brilliant and the breeze kind and strong, varying up to twenty-five knots and pushing us along nicely night and day. The boys had found their sea legs, although Edward had difficulty finding his appetite. All tasks were shared equally, such as cooking, washing up and taking watches. Cooking was not always easy with the boat rolling and the heat intensifying the further south we came. Life had started to become routine and kind in the lovely warm day and night. *Luna Quest* did all the work, straining at the halyards and sheets. The mast groaned a little from time to time, while our little home rolled and hummed under a trade wind sky.

In the morning we would invariably find dolphins darting about our bow and flying fish skimming the waves. From time to time we found one or two on deck. If it had not killed itself in landing it sometimes flipped itself back into the sea. They provided us with great joy and excitement. One night when Philip was on watch he received one right in his chest. It seemed to us that we were gaining on our competitors by the relative positions the participants reported to the class leader at ten a.m. over the SSB radio. Our parasail was clearly doing its magic. Towards the end of the first week, when the wind had picked up to Force Six touching Force Seven, and *Luna Quest* was regularly making nine knots, a speed that was probably in excess of its theoretical hull speed, we had made up for lost time and overtaken many of our competitors, although we could not see them, but knew from the morning roll call. The strong winds produced some mighty seas that came running up behind us, threatening to engulf our little home, but each time the wave would break just shy of the stern, sending her foam either side of the boat. *Luna Quest* almost surfed down the larger ones, with the frothing white water passing at great speed. The sky and ocean remained a brilliant blue. The parasail billowed taut. It was sheer joy to experience the use of these forces of nature, although the motion of the boat could be quite violent at times.

Then we had to hold on with all our might to stop us from risking a fall and injuring ourselves. I was always very much aware of my sore ribcage, avoiding any risk of it being compromised, but my breathing was fine and there was nothing I could not do other than lying on my side. I had taken to using spare pillows and clothes either side of my shoulders and head while my legs were spread out to stop me from being rolled by the boat's motion. It was wonderful to turn in when my watch was up, knowing that *Luna Quest* would carry on being powered by the wind, regardless of who was on watch. It was even more wonderful to wake up to yet another glorious day and find *Luna Quest* playing with the waves as she had done the day before. We never saw a ship or sail or anything manmade, night and day.

Our ablutions were kept to a minimum, given our limited water supply. Hot water was not available, although I had provided the boat with a small electric fresh water maker and a handheld deck shower; a black bag with a tube and a small plastic shower head on the end, which after an hour on deck in the sun would produce a generous amount of warm water. Unfortunately, the first time we tried it, having filled it with fresh water and wedged it on the side deck against the gunwale so that it received maximum sunshine, the sea took it before we even noticed. That was the end of any showering on board.

While our fixed solar panels re-charged our batteries during the day, it seemed that our tricolour sailing light was more power-hungry than our batteries could supply adequate energy for. The further south we sailed, the shorter our days, and the tricolour light now had to stay on for nearly twelve hours. I employed our towed generator during the night to help with the power generation, but the speed of the boat would pull the spinner clear of the water each time a wave passed it. The line holding the spinner would go mad out of the water, turning the opposite way ten times faster and undoing the twist in the line that was meant to turn the generator. At the same time the line would knot itself in various places at great speed so that the benefit of its employment did not outweigh the loss of speed that *Luna Quest* necessarily suffered as a result of the drag the line and spinner caused. We could therefore only deploy it when the wind was less strong, the waves less high and the boat speed reduced.

A yacht sailing goose-winged, but without spinnaker, appeared on our starboard bow. She was very likely to be an ARC participant, although she appeared much bigger than *Luna Quest*. As a participant I would have expected her to be well ahead of us, but we were gaining on her by leaps and bounds. She was sailing under reefed mainsail and genoa, probably making some five knots of speed in the twenty-eight-knots of trade wind, while we were under full parasail, powering along at an average of eight-and-a-half knots. We exchanged waves as we passed, but could not ascertain whether they were a participant. We glorified in this feat of one-upmanship, but at the same time considered whether we, too, should carry less sail. The mast groaned a little more than before and the chafe on the gear became a concern. I checked the gear every day. The sheets showed a little chafe, but the halyard appeared unaffected. Looking at the backstay, I wondered whether the tensioner fitted to it was strong enough. The entire force of the parasail, spread over just three points of the sail, was on this one stainless steel stay that held the mast up and the gear together. If that ruptured, we would lose our mast and all that attached to it. Then we considered that we would not be able to take in the parasail; the upward force on the collar in trying to snuff the sail by pulling it down would be tremendous and, as our previous experience had shown, a very risky exercise! We speculated that we would have to sail past St Lucia because we could not pull the sail down. We laughed and joked about it, but reality would be differently disposed.

We discussed the risks and the pros and cons of sailing at full speed under the billowing parasail and as we had decided that we could not and would not take it down, whatever the wind speed, we just awaited fate to take its course. Perhaps there would be a lull before long, perhaps the trade winds would never exceed forty knots, but as long as the sky was blue, the sea magnificent and the speed marvellous, we did not really worry too much. The wind began to blow more strongly now, sometimes over thirty knots, and the strain on the gear was tremendous. The Hydrovane had difficulty coping and from time to time we had to help it to counteract the swings in the parasail. It would swing from left to right with all the thirty-two knots of wind trying to blow it off the ship. *Luna Quest* rolled quite violently, and if anybody from the Yacht club could see us now, they would be forgiven for thinking that the crew had lost their minds or that the ship was on a desperate mission. Touching thirty-five knots from time to time, the Hydrovane was overpowered. *Luna Quest* began to surf down the massive rollers with big white teeth trying to bite her. Only occasionally would one succeed and wash over the stern into the cockpit. Hand-steering was now required, which proved quite hard. We set watches of ninety minutes. The sailing was as exciting as sailing can be and although perhaps a tad concerned that we were overdoing it, *Luna Quest* did not seem to mind one bit that she was being thrashed across the Atlantic. The gear stood firm, the shrouds as taut as piano strings, and the backstay, the one stay that kept all the other gear intact, hamstrung to its limit.

Our position in the fleet improved by the day. After each roll call we looked forward to the next one, and wondered how much more we had gained on the others. We started to jot down the relative positions and plotted them on the North Atlantic Passage Chart, but the area we were in was too small on the small-scale chart for the entire north Atlantic, so we just did mental arithmetic to calculate how much we had gained. We did not seem to lose on anybody. As we were also overhauling the bigger class boats, we imagined coming across a boat sooner or later. The wind kept blowing a good Force Six and the sensation of winning, together with the white capped breakers all around against a beautiful blue sky, put us in an exhilarating mood. At this rate we might be outpacing the bigger class boats in their entirety! What a benefit that we could not pull the parasail down! *Luna Quest* just bombed along, throwing aside the excess water in her way and creating a distinctive wake. But the strains were clearly too much for *Luna Quest* to bear, for on the seventh day at around five p.m. there was a cannon shot on the foredeck, followed by cries from the cockpit that the parasail was torn and flying like a demented giant flag from the masthead. Scrambling on deck I expected one of the shrouds to have given out under the strain or the mast snapped in two, but instead found the parasail with the port sheet horizontally out from the top of the mast. Some thirty metres of sail and sheet functioned as one in wild twists and gyrations to tell us that they were intent on taking the mast and all its rigging down. They had had enough and the protest was clear. Immediate action was called for.

The collar and sock were still intact at the top of the sail. We began to haul the collar down, which, thank goodness, proved very easy as the sail had completely collapsed into a long twisted dish cloth, flailed about by the high wind. Despite its gyrations, it was greedily gobbled up by the collar and buried in the sock at the slightest pull. Without the collar and sock, we would have had to let the sail fly off its halyard and be blown into the sea for ultimate retrieval. But the collar and sock had proved their worth and all of the parasail came down submissively. We would not be flying that again, and pushed it down the forehatch. We would worry about repairs later. With two reefs in the mainsail and a reefed foresail our speed dropped to five-and-a-half knots, but the boat's motion had become delightfully easy and hand-steering was no longer required. The Hydrovane was back in control. We would not now be making any gain on our competitors, but would rather lose ground. I hoped that we might at least retain our position.

The damage we sustained was limited, but significant. Where we had hooked the whisker pole into an eye on the spinnaker boom itself near the mast, the aluminium fitting on the boom had chafed completely through so that the whisker pole had been sent flying forward by the force of the wind into the parasail, which, because of the huge strain it was under, needed only the touch of something that was unforgiving, like the stainless steel end of the whisker pole, to cause a major rip. In fact the whisker pole caused two major rips. Nature had taken its vengeance on the reckless crew and had shown it to be the master of all forces. That was Sunday, seven days out from Las Palmas. As if to compensate us for the lack of spinnaker, the wind piped up to thirty-five knots on Monday and stayed there. It was just as well we no longer had the parasail up because something else would almost certainly have given out, like a stay or a shroud, as I came to realise on the way back from Antigua! *Luna Quest* revelled in the high winds. Its reefed mainsail and reefed genoa were just perfect to give it maximum hull speed, fully loaded, of seven-and-a-half knots. The rolling had diminished significantly. We no longer had to hold on to anything to remain on our feet, the vibrating had stopped, and the hum only now accompanied a surf down the waves. The sky remained blue with occasional white clouds. How perfect sailing could be! We sat in the cockpit, sunning ourselves and discussing the ways of the world. Despite the high winds we were able to rig the sun canopy over the cockpit, a simple device that zipped on to the sprayhood and fastened aft to the backstay and sun panel frame. We ate well and slept well and were more than surprised to learn at the ten o'clock morning roll call that we were still gaining on the fleet.

I had taken to using the towed generator to supplement the batteries that found it difficult to feed our power-hungry tricolour light. Although fully charged during the day from the solar panels, it was surprising, despite our use of head torches, how much power we used in the near twelve hours of darkness, because the days and the nights in the lower latitudes are almost equally long. However, its use was not a great success. The spinner kept jumping out of the water, unspinning the line to which it was attached by an opposite mad spin and knotting up the line itself. When it dropped back in the next wave, it spun the line back the right way, but failed to deliver any input until the line was fully twisted back and taut enough to spin the generator mounted on the pushpit. I tried lengthening the line, employing weights to the line, but all to no avail. The spinner would not stay in the water. In the morning it took me about an hour to haul in the spinner, unravel the dozens of knots and spins in the line and stow it away. We did not want any unnecessary drag during the day when the solar panels supplied adequate power to replenish the batteries.

One of my daily tasks was to write an email home, relating the events of the day. When we had been powering along under the parasail, it had at times been quite difficult to hit the correct keys on the keyboard of my laptop, but I had got used to it but probably spent as much time correcting typing errors as writing the emails themselves. Now that we were in a reasonably stable boat, despite the Force Seven winds, I thought I would write a decent email to compensate for the summary emails I had been writing under the difficult conditions of the previous week. I set about with all good intentions and wrote quite an extensive report, incorporating experiences that I had put aside before. The email was virtually ready to go and having edited it to make it even more presentable, it suddenly disappeared from the screen by the touch of some key that my fingers much have tapped inadvertently. No matter what efforts I undertook to retrieve it, the frustration grew into an oversized balloon. Of course, it exploded… "No more emails, that's done it, nobody reads them in any case!" and I shut my computer, intending not to use it again. Later on in the day, however, I re-considered: if I did not write any more, they would be worried at home, wondering what we had been up to. So in the afternoon I sat down again and wrote the email afresh with a better result, I thought, than the one composed in the morning. While I was writing it, the boys called me up because another yacht was spotted. As I came up the companionway, poking my head above the parapet of the cockpit, I was amazed to see the yacht so near. It was only maybe half a mile away, heading across our course under a scrap of foresail only. I recognised the boat as the one that had been on our pontoon in Las Palmas. Were we off course or was he? Perhaps he was hove to. I checked our course and the chart and knew our course was spot on. I could not for the life of me understand where the skipper of the yacht thought he was heading unless he had decided to go across the equator into the southern hemisphere, or just hoped the wind would abate before setting sail again on the correct course! The skipper was standing on deck and as we passed we exchanged greetings. To see his boat being lifted up into the sky by a wave and carried in a bath of white foam while we were in the trough of another before being lifted up ourselves, was a truly memorable sight. We were soon out of sight from each other and were not in the least surprised when they checked into St Lucia a week after our arrival!

The high winds were wreaking damage among the participating boats. One, it was reported over the radio, had lost its mast and another two yachts their steering. One of these had lost its rudder blade altogether and was carrying on under a jury rudder. We would hear more about that on their arrival. A fourth boat had lost its entire crew of three to the rescue services as its skipper had suffered a mental breakdown and had to be restrained by his crew of one doctor and a fisherman. The rescue services, however, would not take the skipper off unless the doctor came with him. The fisherman refused to be left alone on the boat and so he, too, was taken off. The boat called 'Compromise' was abandoned and left to drift at the behest of the seas and winds. We had its position and considered salvaging it, but to sail 150 miles back into the Force Seven trade winds seemed a hazardous affair, especially as there was no certainty of finding it. The boat was reported to have washed up in one of the Caribbean islands nearly two months later. It had been stripped of anything of any value, its mast broken and its sails in tatters. Of the crew we heard no more.

Our sailing and progress continued better than expected. We kept overhauling other participants, including the Sigma 40 in the racing division that we had been next to on the pontoon in Las Palmas. The crew must have been seriously gutted to know that we, fully laden with all the goodies on board that Marion had bought for us in ample supplies, our diesel tank full, our water tank full plus dozens of Evian one-litre bottles stowed up forward, our fridge full of fresh foods and hundreds of tins, bottles, sauces, packages of the most palatable foods and bread for lunch, were outrunning them, despite their attempts to keep their weight down. As they were in the racing division, they were not allowed to use their engines and so no diesel had been shipped. The Sigma 40 relied on their water maker only, had denied themselves any food supplies other than freeze dried foods in tiny packages and limited teabags, all in an effort to save on weight! *Luna Quest* did not seem to mind being overweight; she just creamed along at top speed, drawing a perfect great circle on our North Atlantic Passage Chart. I could not but help admiring her sea-kindliness, her determination to plough on towards her goal, shaking off any wave toppings that tumbled on deck. I secretly praised Peter Brett, her designer, for producing such a perfect pocket ocean cruiser. She was no tupperware boat, as sailors generally refer to the lighter, modern plastic craft. She had been strongly built, the last of a successful series started in the 1970s, amended and improved over the years so that by the time her keel was laid in 1986, the cost of her build had far outstripped that of the tupperware boats. *Luna Quest*'s first owner must have been quite a discerning yachtsman with deep pockets to opt for a Rival 38 when he could have bought a larger sailing boat for a lot less money. *Luna Quest*'s mast was decidedly short compared with any mast fitted to a tupperware boat, but I liked that as it gave the impression of seaworthiness, come what may.

The weather in the second week of our voyage continued to produce some good, strong trade winds, but the incidence of squalls became more frequent. We had been warned how to recognise them and assess their strengths. Some of them looked truly ominous with low black clouds, but we had been told that the lower the cloud mass, the less strong the wind, as the cold air within the cloud has not so far to fall. How high low is and how low high is we found out by experience. One thing they had in common was the massive water content that seemed to cease-lessly sweep over the seas in heavy torrents of watery curtains, obliterating the horizon. As we watched their tracks across the ocean we tried to estimate whether we were going to be unlucky and be hit, and whether we would have to shorten sail and how soon. There would be a lull before the downdraught of the squall cloud reached the hapless crew of *Luna Quest*. More often than not they would track a mile or so past us and if they came up from behind we could count on some extra wind. Some of those squalls were quite massive, taking up half the horizon, but then the more massive they appeared, the lower they were and the less bite they appeared to have. One of them, however, gave us nearly forty knots of wind, but *Luna Quest* did not blink a sail. She just increased her speed and enjoyed the dance in a pelted sea. We therefore left her under her reduced canvass, which seemed the right amount of sail no matter what the wind strength was.

The weather had become decidedly hotter, night and day. It was a great temptation to strip off, but the strength of the sun and our fear of skin damage kept us covered in the most basic of coverings. Our little awning over the cockpit did its best to give us protection, but the rolling and the heeling marginalised its effect. In any case, it was better than not having one at all. Edward kept to his bunk most of the time as his sea legs had failed to develop, but if there was a job to be done, he would manly discharge the task, including his turn for cooking or washing up. He had visibly lost some weight, but refused to take any Stugeron, an anti-seasickness tablet, hoping always that his body system would adjust in due course. Philip spent most of his time in the cockpit, enjoying the weather and the scenery. Schools of flying fish zipped over the waves, providing a constant joy to watch. There would always be one or two on deck first thing in the morning.

The weather into the third week must have been disturbed by some frontal system as the wind dropped to Force Two to Three. There was much pleading by the crew to put the engine on, but I considered that a violation of nature's peace and quiet and allowed *Luna Quest* to find her own pace. Eventually, some wind returned, lifting our spirits and making us think about landfall, but the winds stayed feeble for many days. As we were drifting at about three knots in a westerly direction, a large spinnaker appeared on the horizon behind us. It was the first time we had spotted a boat behind us and this one was making on us; the spinnaker grew larger by the minute. We cursed the damage to our own and wished we could hoist a replacement spinnaker to give fair chase to the yacht coming up behind. It was clearly interested in investigating us as it passed quite closely. She proved nearly twice our size with a spinnaker three times our parasail and carrying a crew of fourteen. We cleared our throats, adjusted our binoculars, feeling less embarrassed than when we first saw her appear on the horizon. The day before our arrival in St Lucia the wind fell away to a light breeze. We were determined to keep the pace on without using the engine and hoisted the large loose lightweight genny and set it out on the second telescopic extension of the spinnaker boom (its maximum extension). It looked a little precarious, with the boom flexing in the middle every time the boat's downward motion was arrested by a new swell that lifted her, but we risked leaving it up at night fall in an effort to keep the yacht going as fast as possible under sail. It was a hazardous affair at night. You could not see any squalls coming up and certainly could not know what strength of wind they might have. One day there was a lull in the gentle breeze and, having been lulled into a sense of semi-comatose as a result of the heat and the undulating seas, a nasty little squall suddenly hit us with twenty-four knots of wind sending *Luna Quest* gambolling along at great speed and producing a most fearful bend in the fully extended spin-naker boom. It blew too hard to contemplate taking the lightweight genny in so that all we could do was await another sail rendered. Then, just as suddenly as the squall had arrived, it vanished, leaving us rolling in an awkward sea without wind and the sail flapping. I breathed a sigh of relief for seeing all the gear still intact. When at last we came into Rodney Bay at about eleven p.m., on the nineteenth day out from Las Palmas, we were met by a tumultuous welcome from those who had beaten us to it. They came out in little dinghies and launches, spraying champagne and throwing confetti over us, shouting we had come third in our class. Marion was amongst them, with Christine and Donald doing their best to deliver their congratulations amongst all the shouting. The majority of the welcomers, however, were from the big-boat classes, who had been tracking our incredible progress on their screens. Tired but happy, we found our slot in the marina and crashed out.

We had made the crossing in nineteen days, won third prize in our class, which would have been second if we had motored in the last week as everybody else had done in our class and other classes, sustained only one damaged sail, had four-fifths of our food supply intact and carried all of our diesel fuel in a full tank. I estimated that if we had not overloaded ourselves with food supplies and had not lost twenty-four hours on the first day out from Las Palmas, and had employed the engine during the last week, we would without a shadow of a doubt have been first in our class and well up in the medium-sized class. We would have achieved the crossing in a maximum of seventeen days. We had in any case beaten the Sigma 40 by two days. Towing the generator had been another unnecessary drag. *Luna Quest* had proved herself to be an excellent sea boat, strong and sea kindly. We would experience the benefit of her superb sea-keeping qualities on the way back to England some months later.

PART 3

OUR WANDERINGS IN THE CARIBBEAN

Chapter 11

A taste of St Lucia

Christmas was going to be spent in St Lucia and none of us had any idea of how that might be celebrated, but the Bay Garden Hotel in Rodney Bay, where we had booked ourselves into until the New Year, did its best to produce the Christmas spirit by bringing out lots of well used and ageing decorations. On Christmas Day the hotel manager, dressed in a traditional red woolly Father Christmas outfit, complete with cotton beard, white-plumed red woolly hat and black boots, had cast himself in the additional role of jester. The poor man clearly was not used to being overdressed for he was sweating profusely whilst prancing around the swimming pool under the blazing sun. Some of the British ARC participants had also booked themselves into the hotel for the occasion, helping to make the annual celebration reasonably reminiscent of Christmas at home. Donald and Christine dressed up to go to a tin-roofed church to hear the local priest edifying his flock. They were kept there rather longer than any service at home might have done, but they reappeared unscathed, although somewhat subdued and sleepy. After Christmas they flew home, as did Philip and his sister, who had flown out to St Lucia to be part of the welcoming party.

Graham and Sheila McCartney, who had made the crossing of the Atlantic in their Westerly 37, had some of their children and elderly parents join them in St Lucia to share the celebrations. To provide their family with a taste of how wonderful the sailing was in that part of the world compared with UK waters, they set off on Sunday, 1st January, for Martinique, some twenty miles to the north of St Lucia. The trade winds were quite blustery from the north-east and had been blowing strongly for well over a week, setting up a pronounced swell between the islands. We all waved them a good passage, promising to meet up in due course, but the wind must have blown rather more forcibly than expected or the waves been rather more uncomfortable for they were back within four hours with all but one having become badly seasick.

A day later Marion and I set off south, down the west side of St Lucia to visit Marigot Bay, only seven miles away and so enticingly portrayed on the front cover of the North Atlantic Crossing Guide. Under reefed foresail and no mainsail and in the lee of the island we sped down the edge of the tropical rainforest that skirted the rock-strewn and wild coast of the island. Marigot Bay was as enchanting as the picture on the front cover, but too hot in the shelter of the forested mountains. The natural beauty of it, though, was breathtaking, with the mangrove trees forming an impenetrable hem around the bay, where a few yachts were at anchor. A Norwegian forty-four-footer with a large rubber dinghy bobbing on its port side were anchored next to us. I was not looking forward to extracting our own dinghy from the forecastle, blowing it up and hoisting it off the deck to launch it for what might prove to be only a short visit, and wondered if our neighbours could offer us a lift. They were delighted to make our acquaintance and readily offered their help. Inevitably, we ended up sharing the evening dinner table and learning Norwegian from the elderly professor skipper. Suddenly and thankfully, a massive tropical downpour obliterated any attempt to communicate, which offered me an excuse for not listening to the gobbledegook mumblings from across the table. On the way back to the boat, and clambering on to *Luna Quest*, Marion slipped on the wet cockpit coaming, injuring her knee. It swelled up two days later following another clamber but no slipping, causing her considerable pain and near immobility. We decided to sail back to Rodney Bay as soon as possible and see a doctor before the weekend. Friday morning at 0700hrs we motored out of the bay and ran back fast on the engine before the wind had time to increase in strength with the rising sun. We were back at 0900hrs and with the help of a walking stick and taxi we managed to see Dr Beaubrun in Rodney Bay, who had prescribed Marion medicine some weeks earlier for a chest infection. Now on strong painkillers we hoped recovery might set in, but the following day the pain seemed worse and Marion could not move from her bunk. I scoured the town for crutches and eventually found the only pair, an old-fashioned design with arm rests. I also booked us back into the Bay Garden Hotel, where our room looked out over the garden and the pool. I was pleased that Marion could now relax and give her knee time to settle down. Various doctors on holiday in the hotel came over to express their diagnosis and cure, which, much to our surprise, varied from one to the next. One thing we did learn was that the knee was a very complicated piece of articulation, where it was often difficult to establish exactly what was wrong with and what was best for the knee. We decided to let the knee rest and fly home as soon as Marion became a little more mobile. A fortnight later we booked our flights home to England, Marion in business class with her leg up and me in steerage.

On 11th February we flew back to Rodney Bay with four reasonably good knees. Rather than sailing south to the Grenadine islands, we booked ourselves a daytrip to Union Island. An old Britten Norman B2, seating eight guests, rattled us down azure blue seas and tropical islands. On arrival a cockroach-infested wooden schooner-type vessel took us to the white sand beaches of the uninhabited islands of Palm Island, Mayreau and Tobago Quays. In Mayreau a cruise ship was busy landing its passengers for a laid-on lunch set out on many trestle

Marigot Bay, St. Lucia

tables. A few yachtsmen and our crew that mingled with the cruise ship passengers in the tiny island could have helped themselves freely to any of the lunch or drinks set out by the cruise ship as there did not appear to be any security or a facility to pay. Unfortunately, we already had our lunch, but I could not resist the temptation to test the system and asked for a soft drink. It was immediately proffered with a polite smile and wishes to enjoy a good day. Whilst Marion was sunning herself on the beach I went to explore the innards of the island. I could not have gone for more than five minutes when I perceived a crude metal fence. It appeared to run right across the island. I then realised that the cruise ship had been able to provide lunch for its guests in the fenced-off, private side of the island for the benefit and security of its passengers, preventing any locals from other islands penetrating the area. However, a little way off and across the fence I noticed what looked like debris. How could there be debris in this paradise island? On closer inspection I found it to be a big garbage dump with black bin liners, plastic bottles and other non-biodegradable rubbish all heaped up in a shallow dug-out. Shocked by the sight of this crime, I realised that the cruise ship would probably have some arrangement in place on paper with the locals from nearby islands for the disposal of the rubbish left on the 'uninhabited and virginal' island after the sumptuous lunch for its passengers, not knowing that in reality the debris would not be disposed of in an eco-friendly manner.

Chapter 12

Island hopping

On Tuesday, 15th February 2007, Marion and I set off for Martinique at 1030hrs from the shelter of Rodney Bay. Our destination was Marin Yacht Harbour, where friends owning a fifty-four-foot Discovery were expecting us. Marion braved a nervous anticipation of instant capsize and foundering as soon as we were around Pidgeon Island, the north-eastern peninsula of St Lucia. Soon we were into the straits between St Lucia and Martinique. The wind blew a fresh breeze to give us an exhilarating sail with the wind on the beam. Despite my efforts to persuade her to sit with me on the lee side of the deep and secure cockpit to enjoy a comfortable passage, she insisted on staying below in the saloon, considering it might be safer in the womb of the ship than out in the cockpit where the wind and the sight of the waves would add to her anxieties. The seas off the island can be a little irregular, and unless one is securely sat down, a rogue wave could cause one to be lurched about. I was a little surprised at her nervousness as it was not the first time she had been on a boat with me. For twenty years we had kept *Sally* in West Mersea and Tollesbury, sailing the east coast rivers with and without the children. She had sailed with me through the canals in Holland and across the Flevolake, which used to be the Zuiderzee in Holland, and although nervous at times because of mishaps or unexpected changes in the weather, she had always managed to overcome her fears and appreciate the virtues of boating. She had even successfully completed an RYA day-skipper's course on the east coast rivers. However, considering that the Atlantic swell and wave heights were very much greater than anywhere in the canals and lakes of Holland, or even around the east coast of England, I suppose the beautiful Caribbean weather with cumulus woolly white clouds and radiant intermittent sun were not enough to help overcome her fears of seeing the waves as aggressive monsters intent on sending *Luna Quest* to the deep.

Suddenly, a larger than average wave gave *Luna Quest* an unexpected lurch, causing Marion to be hurtled towards the cooker on the lee side. Loud cursing and deprecatory cries helped her come up the companionway to give vent to her complaints. Her face spoke of great fear, accusation and agony. She lamented loudly that she could not move from the position she was in, as the boat was at an angle. She would not sit on a sloping seat and therefore remained stuck where she was. Eventually, however, she managed to dislodge herself from that position and struggled into the cockpit like a wounded duck where she immediately, despite my pleadings to join me on the lee side, made for the weather side, high above the sea. She was holding on to the winches with all her might, but soon tired of that and of being sprayed by crashing bow waves. She began to see the advantages of sitting on the lee side, where it was dry, warm and secure. She chose her moment to aim and then launched her bottom on to the lee side cockpit seat. Yes, that was much more comfortable, but now the water was much nearer to her, causing her to take fright once again. She decided she would be better off down below in the saloon. The white clouds over St Lucia had now made way for brilliant sunshine over a blue sea with occasional white caps. This was the sailing that coastal yachtsmen around England could only dream of.

We found our friends in Marin Yacht Harbour in none too happy a mood. Domestic problems at home and on board put a dark edge to their holiday spirits and made it difficult for us to enjoy their company. Her skipper was keen to get to Antigua, but his wife wanted to get home to sort out a wayward daughter. Marion was keen to go home and sail no more and I was keen to get on with the sailing. Despite our various differences, the wives were persuaded to stay and accompany their husbands the following day in the lee of the island to St Pierre on the north-west side of the island from where we could hop across to Portsmouth in Rupert Bay, Dominica. Marion was very hesitant, but the promise of a smooth sea behind the island convinced her that this time she would not be so frightened. The morning broke propitiously; the sun was out in a cloudless sky and the sea as smooth as a polished table top. Marion was looking forward to the trip and once cast off she found herself surprised at how enjoyable the trip promised to be. She got the camera out and took at least half a dozen shots of a solitary rock called Diamond Rock as we sailed in between it and Martinique. My promise of a smooth sea held and we arrived in the middle of the afternoon. The next leg, however, would be some sixty miles further north, a long day's sail and across an open stretch of water between Martinique and Dominica. Marion had wobbles. Our friends suggested she joined the Discovery, stressing that she did not have to make a decision there and then, but could sleep on it and that he would be happy to receive her decision at any time before *Luna Quest* was due to set off for Dominica early in the morning. It would certainly be an early start for *Luna Quest*, definitely not later than 0700hrs if I wanted to arrive at our destination before nightfall, whereas our friends could leave a little later as their boat would make much faster passage, being a bigger boat. By nature, Marion is not given to making quick decisions, so that the time she had been allowed to think about it caused her some distress and all night she tossed and turned, trying to make up her mind. On the one hand she felt she was letting me down, but on the other, the prospect of a steady sail in company of another female with all the luxury on board as shown in glossy magazines, was a temptation that worked as powerfully on her as the North Pole works on the needle of a compass. At 0600hrs the alarm went off, followed by more indecision. Our friends were still asleep, but I had to get going at 0700hrs at the latest. She called our friends on the VHF. Not letting on that such an early call might have been a trifle irritating, the skipper generously forgave her and welcomed her aboard his yacht. He was over in five minutes and took Marion off.

After a hasty breakfast and a shallow squall, I set off at 0700hrs under a leaden sky, a little drizzle and little wind. However, as soon as I was in between islands, the trade wind belted in from the east rising to twenty-seven knots in another passing squall. *Luna Quest* was under full sail and her toerail dipped under water in protest. We sailed as fast as *Luna Quest* could manage. After a couple of hours we were in the lee of Dominica, where the wind suddenly dropped to a Force Three. Our progress was now slow and I saw the fifty-four-foot Discovery coming up fast behind me. I was determined to stay ahead of her and arrive at Rupert Bay before they did, but the wind continued fickle and my sails proved too small. In overtaking me, the crew of the Discovery waved and took pictures of *Luna Quest*. Then she was past. On arrival in the bay, I passed our friends at anchor and dropped mine in shallower water, closer to the coast. Marion reported that she had had a wonderfully easy passage with breakfast and lunch in the cockpit. She gave a glowing account of the smooth sail she had experienced in a 'proper' boat, whose sails rolled up or out on command by the press of a button and where the boat seemed to stay upright, including the drinks on the cockpit table. I recalled my own lunch of a couple of slices of bread downed by half a bottle of stale wine left over from the night before, but I was glad Marion had had an enjoyable trip.

She had now regained sufficient confidence to consent to staying on *Luna Quest* for the short hop across to Les Saintes, a small group of islands just south of Guadeloupe. So as not to cause her alarm when hauling up the anchor, I explained the procedure, which includes having to disperse from time to time the incoming chain into the anchor locker from the capstan to stop the chain from heaping up like a pyramid inside it and blocking the naval pipe through which the chain enters the boat, because once the pipe is blocked, the capstan cannot get rid of the incoming chain and stops. I use for the purpose of spreading the chain a stout piece of wood, which I take down into the anchor locker whilst the capstan is doing its work. I explained to Marion the various actions involved, including having to dive down into the anchor chain locker from time to time to disperse the chain. As I weighed anchor, Marion, sitting in the cockpit, was seized by a panic attack, accusing me of utter incompetence in taking so long getting the anchor up when everybody else seemed to have taken no time at all. I explained again how I needed to disperse the anchor chain heaping up in the anchor locker, but she would have none of it and allowed herself to be overtaken by morbid fear of instant sinking, but the anchor came up nicely and once stowed she calmed down and we could motor out into the lee side of the island towards the gap between this island and the next, Les Saintes. I hoisted the mainsail with a reef in it, expecting a little more wind in the gap. A twenty knot trade wind now jumped into our sails and lay *Luna Quest* over at a twenty degree angle. This put Marion in another panic attack, cursing the boat, me and the sailing. She said she hated sailing and wanted to get off as fast as possible. I put a reef in the genny to complement the reef in the mainsail. Then the wind died and we motored the rest of the way. The boat being upright restored Marion's confidence and it looked as though she was enjoying herself again. We passed through a narrow gap between outlying satellite islands and came upon a large bay protected from the trade winds by semi-mountainous islands all round. However, we were not alone. There were quite a few yachts dotted around at anchor and we quickly appreciated the bay's appeal. The crystal clear water and the sandy bottom with fish darting about offered a peaceful attraction and invited complete rest. I decided to go as near to the land as was physically possible and after some manoeuvring I managed to pick up the one and only mooring buoy in the bay. Clearly, no other boat had deemed the buoy safe enough to tie up to or out of courtesy to its owner had simply passed it. A skipper nearby reassured us that the buoy had not been used for as long as he had been there, adding that he could think of no reason why anybody had not tied up to it yet.

It was in an ideal location, quite close to the shore, but in a good twelve feet of water. A dinghy, however, would nevertheless be required, together with a good outboard to get us ashore, perhaps only two minutes away. I had not had a need for the dinghy's use since leaving Turkey as we had been sailing from marina to marina, but now that we were at anchor an opportunity had presented itself to test it. I had had it and the outboard serviced in Turkey, so was reasonably confident that both would work, but it was a new experience for me to get it ready and launch it off *Luna Quest*'s deck. I had seen other yachtsmen use their halyards to help them lower their dinghies into the water and I determined to try the same. It had lived in a fold-up state on one of the forepeak berths since leaving Turkey, but to get it ready meant having to carry it through the saloon and up the companionway. This is no mean feat. After much huffing and puffing I managed to get it on deck, where I found that the only place I might expect it to fully unfold was on the bit of foredeck right above the hatchway. Once that was achieved, there was very little room for standing space. In attempting to attach the air pump's plastic hose to the nozzle on the dinghy, I found that its age had taken the life out of the plastic so that it simply brittled away. Without a hose that could connect the air pump to the air chambers in the dinghy, there would be no going ashore. I cut a piece off, wound some tape around the new end and tried again. It worked and away we pumped. Slowly, the dinghy inflated, taking the shape I had seen in Turkey. Once blown up, I used the spinnaker halyard to hoist it partially above the lifelines, which now seemed anything but protective. They were hard and hazardous fittings for the thin rubberised material the dinghy was made from. I pushed it over the lifelines, let it dangle against them and slowly lowered it into the water. I realised that if there had been any wind, I would have had little chance of getting it into the water at all. I hoped such an occasion would not arise. Once she bobbed in the water, cosying up to *Luna Quest*, I attached the outboard to a swing hoist that I had had especially made for the purpose in Turkey to overcome the potential problem of not being able to get the outboard into the dinghy without causing damage to *Luna Quest*'s topsides. The hoist worked a treat and the outboard was lowered on to the transom of the dinghy effortlessly. A couple of pulls and the outboard sprang into life, but it did not sound happy and I would have to give it a good look-over in the morning, but for now I would just have to hope that she did not conk out halfway to the shore. As luck would have it we made it ashore without any hiccup. However, on the way back the engine did conk out, resulting in me having to row the remainder of the way back to *Luna Quest*.

The following morning I set to work. My weight in the back of the dinghy and my leaning over the engine caused the dinghy to rear its head, threatening to swamp me in the stern. If I moved very carefully, however, I could just about avoid causing the rear of the dinghy to ship water. I removed a bolt from the carburettor, which decided to lose itself over the stern and into the deep. I could not carry on like this. There would be more accidents. The engine needed to be on a work bench, high and dry. I climbed back on *Luna Quest* and called the yacht club recommended in the pilot guide as a helpful resource for skippers in trouble. Jerome, its owner, said that there was no engineer about, but that his wife could do all our washing and that he could supply me with fresh water. Visualising a smart and expensive establishment, and hoping we might find some member with engineering skills in the club, we piled our laundry into the dinghy and set off rowing across the bay, perhaps a mile across. It was difficult rowing because I had not twigged how to secure the oars properly into their rowlocks. All the time I worried about breaking the rubber thole fittings that bent over more and more ominously. The weight in the dinghy was too great and the wind too strong. Luckily, we passed a pontoon that jutted out into the bay, where we could rest and regain our breath. Marion volunteered to get off and walk the rest of the way to lighten the boat. I carried on rowing, stopping every now and again and resting on an occasional anchor chain or a moored boat, avoiding those that were attached to boats that seemed unoccupied. Eventually I reached the 'Yacht club'. At home we have some very smart yacht clubs and we have very modest ones. Some, indeed, could do with a lick of paint, such as the one at Hollowshore at the end of Oare Creek, near Faversham, but this yacht club could not be identified other than by a notice hung loosely over a languid beach bar, showing the word 'Yachtclub', with a loutish Frenchman, Jerome, behind it, chatting up two American blondes, while his morose wife busied herself sorting out our laundry. It seemed Jerome's place was the only place on that side of the island. There were no boating facilities whatsoever, let alone any evidence of a yacht club. A vicious-looking Alsatian barked maliciously at Marion when she asked the wife if she might use the toilet. Having offloaded the laundry, I found the end of a hose tied to a solitary buoy off the beach, which I assumed to be the fresh water supply. I called Jerome to turn the water on and, having made sure any stale water in the pipe had been wasted, I filled our tank before paddling rather than rowing back, so as not to put unnecessary strain on the rowlocks. Although Marion did not have the continued strength to help me paddle, she had the wit to hail a nearby British ensign at anchor with its dinghy tied up at the stern. She requested the skipper for a lift, to which, much to my surprise, the young occupant couple consented. They towed us in their motorised tender to the nearest jetty, where Marion spotted a very flash powerboat that was about to set off. Again she hailed them and obligingly the two men on board towed us all the way back to *Luna Quest*. "No problem," they said and roared off.

Having lost only one screw, which I managed to replace with a similar one from my onboard supplies, I considered that I ought to be able to cure the outboard problem myself if I had a counterweight in the bow. Being now properly prepared, I dismantled the fuel system, carefully placing each nut and bolt in the bottom of the dinghy, blew it through and fitted it back again. A couple of pulls and the engine sprang to life. Triumphantly, I set off around *Luna Quest*, not too far, just in case. Then it stalled and no matter how many times I pulled, it was as dead as a doornail. The tide was steadfastly carrying me towards the open sea, but I was not worried as I had some good oars with me. Marion had been watching the proceedings from the cockpit and visualised the loss of her husband, absorbed in pulling the starter cord time after time whilst slowly but inexorably being carried out to sea. I looked up to give myself a relief from the pouring sweat and a rest to my aching right arm. I saw Marion gesticulating and hailing the skipper of a large and impressive French motor yacht anchored nearby, making it known to him through sign language the predicament her husband had got himself in. I protested by voice that I was all right, but it was too late for the Frenchman was already upon me in his dinghy. He obligingly suggested that my fuel was dirty and I change it. He could well be right as I had not used any of it since Turkey. He said he had plenty of it, offering it to me whilst towing me back to *Luna Quest*, which rode peacefully at anchor. She unquestionably offered her motherly security to her little blown-up rubber child, which soon bobbed happily beside her. On the Frenchman's advice, I unscrewed the drain plug, losing it instantly to the deep of the crystal-clean, clear waters of the bay. Without the drain plug, a little petrol spilled out of the system that instantly corrupted the serenity of the beautiful waters. The speed at which it spread was alarming. I have seen bushfires fanned by strong winds eat up vegetation voraciously, but how a little petrol can spread so fast and so far without any continued source for its supply, gave me visions of culpable damage and the forfeiture of *Luna Quest*. But nobody noticed and after a while the dissipation caused a gap of clear water between *Luna Quest* and the slick. Immediate guilt subsided. I looked around to see who else might be blamed by association, but the slick was now so thinly spread that the threat of environmental damage had dissipated with it. The Frenchman had not noticed either. I did not have a spare drain plug and wondered if the Frenchman might be able to oblige. I rowed over to him, knocked on the boat, thanked him for his kindness for bringing me back to *Luna Quest* and asked him about the plug. His kindness was unbounded and he obligingly offered to let me rummage through his chest of spares on board his well-equipped boat. He helped me with the search. When we could not find a suitable replacement plug he offered to take me in his tender to the local hardware store in search of a new one. He said he was going there in any case. In the store he helped me look for a new plug and much to our surprise we found one. I was mightily relieved, not so much because we had found a replacement plug, but because my feelings of guilt had been building strongly during the search and were on the edge of brimming over their reservoir whilst I was thinking about how I was wasting the Frenchman's time through utter incompetence. Once out of the shop my mind raced around trying to think of what might have caused the engine to stall, when it suddenly dawned on me that unless air was allowed into the tank as petrol was used, a vacuum would stop the flow of fuel into the carburettor. Back on board I opened the valve on top of the petrol tank and whoosh, the engine roared into action.

On Thursday 1st March 2007 we said goodbye to our Frenchman, his family and the lovely Isles de Saintes and headed for Deshaies in the north of Guadeloupe, towing the dinghy for the first time. The winds and the motion of *Luna Quest* were kind. It was only twenty-five miles and most of that distance was in the lee of Guadeloupe. Marion's nerves held. We dropped anchor in the bay of Deshaies at 1315hrs, where the winds came howling down the mountains in true katabatic fashion, creating in the process the most alarming noise. Judging by the force of these winds, one might have thought that there was a full gale raging out in the open sea whereas, I was convinced, there was no more than a Force Four. Because of the unpredictability of these winds I decided to put a second anchor out on a chum to stop *Luna Quest* from being involuntarily swung around and hitting the boat next door on our port side. She was a smaller boat, a bit tatty and had a Belgian ensign on the stern. There was not a great deal of room between us or between us and the boat that had come to anchor on our starboard side. I felt confident that the two anchors would keep *Luna Quest* in her place and stop her from becoming a threat to her neighbours. The new arrival was an old fashioned classic from England, whose skipper had probably spotted our red duster and thought that *Luna Quest* would offer safe companionship. After he had dropped his hook in the fading light of day he fiddled with his anchor winch on the foredeck for some considerable time. I thought of *Sally*, where bits of equipment through age have a tendency not to perform the function when you most need them. I hoped he would be all right in the morning. We had not long turned in when towards midnight we were woken up by loud banging on our pushpit. The crew on the Belgian boat next to us were desperately trying to wake us up and draw our attention to the imminent danger of collision. My sleepy head could not grasp the situation immediately, but it was obvious that action was called for. I looked around and found that the wind had turned 180 degrees, with nearly every boat having swung around on the full length of their cables except *Luna Quest*, which had held firm on its two anchors. I could not see the point of entering into any discussion with the skipper of the Belgian boat since having anchored after they had, the unwritten rule among skippers of 'last in, first out' applied to me as far as they were concerned. The classic boat appeared unaware of the howling wind or the predicament it had put me and itself in. By anchoring elsewhere I would solve two problems in one. I therefore decided to get into action quickly before serious damage was done. I winched up the second anchor first, spending some considerable time disengaging it from the chum. Once freed, the anchor chain came up easily, but as it tightened, it made *Luna Quest* spin around. Perhaps it was the katabatic winds that howled down or tidal eddies, but she spun around like a conker on a piece of string. I feared she would bash into the Belgian boat and then into the classic boat but she missed them by a couple of feet. The faster I hauled in the anchor chain, the faster she would make concentric circles. Soon, however, the danger of collision appeared past as she had now missed the two neighbours twice in her wild may-tree dance. I hauled in the rest of the chain as fast as I could with *Luna Quest* going around in ever smaller circles. Why she danced this merry-go-round has remained a puzzle. She never did it again. If I had bashed into either boat, I wonder who would have been liable. I motored off in the dead of night towards the outer edges of the bay, where we dropped anchor in deep water. I then sat outside for about an hour, watching *Luna Quest*'s movements. The anchor seemed to hold. The wind had abated and so I turned in and slept until a new howl of the wind woke me up at about 0830hrs the following morning.

I found myself now more in the middle of the bay towards its outer edges where the katabatic winds seemed to be less fierce. But just after nightfall on the second day, the winds howled again in great fury. Playing Cosi von Tuti helped to blot out this fearful noise and to imagine ourselves in a vast opera house. On the morning of the third day a beautiful two-masted classic yacht was trying to sail off his anchor at about the time the katabatic winds had a habit of falling off the mountains. He was anchored right on the edge of the bay, where the seabed is reported to fall off steeply to immeasurable ocean depths. His mainsail was hoisted fully and hauled tight in, as one would expect to keep the boat's head into the wind, but the wind somehow got hold of it and pushed the boat around like a cork in a pond. The skipper thought to solve the problem by easing the main-sheet, but she now lay over in the strengthening wind and wanting to dash off at full speed, dragging the anchor chain alongside. Luckily, the nearest boat was some way off. The skipper realised that sailing off the anchor was not going to work without engine power and, having brought his yacht up into the wind with the help of his engine, he now hauled the sail in tight again and set about again weighing anchor. At last he was off. Another yacht anchored near to the shore, prepared to get underway. It looked an ideal position and before anybody else had similar thoughts I prepared to re-anchor where he had been. The bay there was shallow and I could see the anchor lying on the bottom. We were now the closest of all boats to the shore. It was a wonderful spot, where a visual anchor check could be maintained. Alas, just as we beginning to enjoy this ideal spot we would be on our way to Antigua the following morning. The dark evening clouds chased over the island; a weather forecast could not be obtained. I decided to risk it and set off in any case. In the morning the dark clouds seemed darker and more densely packed than ever before, but we were soon underway into the open sea where the clouds broke up to show us a glorious sky. *Luna Quest* performed beautifully in the Force Four winds, but Marion hated everything about the sailing and the boat and could not wait for her ordeal to end. It was a sad sight to see my otherwise composed wife in such a state of pain and panic. I decided that the boat was no place for her and that I could not have her on the boat again unless we were in a marina having the joy of friends sharing a drink or a meal.

We arrived in the afternoon, exploring the charming and ancient English Harbour of Antigua before dropping anchor in the large bay of Falmouth Harbour. There was an intense buzz about the narrow strip of land that separates English Harbour from Falmouth Harbour. A gathering of the most exquisitely beautiful classic yachts were making preparations for Antigua Classic Week. Several classics invited me to join the crew, including the boat that anchored next us in Deshaies. The paid crews of the larger yachts were washing, polishing, rubbing or re-varnishing. All the boats looked splendid and I was greatly tempted to join one of them. I strolled along the pontoons in great admiration of them all. Seeing those lovely boats and considering their return voyages to Europe or North America to avoid the hurricane season in the Caribbean, I was giving more and more attention to my own return voyage from Antigua to Falmouth in England, weighing up the pros and cons of taking crew. There were many little adverts pinned around the cafes by crew seeking a home passage, and as many stories circulating of unreliable and druggy crew. I decided to do nothing and await events. Brian Taylor, a fifty-nine-year old shipwright and owner of a lovingly restored smack by his own hands, called Rhoda, whom I had met earlier on a friend's boat in Falmouth Harbour, had come to the realisation that his boat was not fit for the return voyage to England. Instead he hoped to sell her during Classic Week and if that were achieved he would love to come back with me. I was half considering undertaking the return on my own, but would be glad to take Brian if available. For a break from his daily chores of rubbing and varnishing, I asked him to join *Luna Quest* to Jolly Harbour in Antigua where I had made arrangements to leave her whilst I flew home with Marion. It was only a short trip of perhaps seven miles, but I became concerned about Brian's seamanship and navigational skills, when he could neither keep course nor read or understand my paper Imray charts. However, I thought no more of it and flew home with Marion.

English Harbour, Antigua

On my return to Antigua I booked myself into the Admiral's Inn and had *Luna Quest* hauled out for a fresh coat of antifouling. I joined the little classic for the five days' racing and enjoyed every minute of it. The participating yachts were just stunning, as were the crews in their boat-specific uniform clothing, reminiscent of the 1930s with a competitive spirit no less keen. Every day produced a glorious regatta of the world's most beautiful boats while the evenings were filled with yarns, drink and laughter. In the meantime Brian had kept up his varnishing work and his hope of finding an interested buyer, but by the end of the week he had not had any interest. I began to worry that I might have to sail back to England on my own as I was reluctant to respond to any of the little adverts pinned around. I persuaded Brian to think that he would be very lucky to sell his boat so quickly and that Rhoda would be better off strapped down on the concrete in the Jolly Harbour's boat yard during the hurricane season. He agreed and a few days later we sailed Rhoda into Jolly Harbour where arrangements for her lay-up were made. I now had the certainty of a crew and Brian a better chance of selling his boat in due course.

The Caribbean

PART 4

A LONG SAIL BACK

Chapter 13

Antigua to Bermuda

The five-month-long hurricane season commences at the beginning of June, but weather patterns in recent years had become unpredictable and most of the yachts that had come to participate in the Antigua Classic Week or in the Antigua Race Week earlier in April had already left for safer waters. Many had been shipped to their home ports rather than sailed home, their skippers fearing the westerly gales on the return voyages in the higher latitudes. Jolly Harbour seemed deserted and, remembering the advice of my old sailing friend, Alastair, who had crossed the Atlantic twice before me, single-handed and in craft much less seaworthy than most, "When in May get away," I was now possessed of a measure of urgency to heed that advice. Brian had taken charge of the provisioning, and several trips were made to the local supermarket with or without my assistance. Many different foods, spices and ingredients that I had never seen before were carefully stowed. Of course, the Caribbean islands are not provisioned on a daily basis and given that so many yachts that had already departed would have cleared the few stores out of all of the most popular food-stuffs, I think that Brian deserved an instant promotion to chief purser, cook and galley boy. He accepted the honour gracefully, provided I would assist with the washing up, a task I undertook unhesitatingly, given that I could then economise on water usage. *Luna Quest* carried only one water tank and no hot water other than that from the kettle. The washing up would have to be undertaken mostly in sea water, followed by a fleeting fresh water rinse. I intended the watermaker to be strictly on standby.

On Monday, 30th April, 2007, after a good lunch ashore, we motored slowly out of Jolly Harbour, glad to be leaving now that it had emptied of boats and feeling hotter than at any time before. Of course, it would become a lot hotter with every day closer to June. Gliding past the many holiday houses built for the Americans along the many manmade waterways out of the harbour seemed unreal. The houses, built of brick and boards, looked flimsy and vulnerable, and especially their little motor boats that every house seemed to have, moored up and seemingly abandoned, sometimes on stilts or in gantries near the verandas. There were very few cars in sight and not a soul to be seen. How would these craft survive if 130mph winds were bent on flying them across the island like kites in the sky? The gardens would be flooded, as might some of the houses. Trees would be uprooted, but there had not been a hurricane in Antigua for many years, and a false sense of security had enticed new wealth to build a raft of these homes. The price of a patch of land ran into multiples of six-figure sums.

The open sea was now in sight and the focus of our attention changed direction. How much wind was there out there? Should we hoist the sails now while still under engine and put a reef in for safety's sake? We remained undecided. Soon we were out to sea. A squally Force Five wind greeted us, gusting up to thirty-five knots. We put *Luna Quest* on a northerly course to pass Barbuda, the last of the Caribbean islands due north. The trade wind came in from the east-north-east, which meant sailing close-hauled. *Luna Quest* under full sail ran at her maximum speed, groaning, her running rigging being stretched to the limit. I realised we were carrying too much sail, but I was keen to get past Barbuda in daylight. I felt a keen mixture of joy, anxiety and exhilaration as we cleared the last of Antigua and headed out for the open Atlantic towards Barbuda. Brian had taken to his bunk, feeling unwell. The wind had settled down to a steady Force Five, but we were not going to get past Barbuda in daylight. Night fell quickly at six o'clock. I put a reef in for the night. A single light ahead indicated the location of the island. The solitary light came nearer and nearer, giving me little rest to think about cooking a meal, being too busy trying to avoid the Barbuda reefs. I had hoped that Brian might recover once out in the Atlantic proper with its unobstructed, easier swell and that we might sit down to our first supper at sea prepared by him.

It was well into the night by the time we cleared Barbuda. The swell had become more regular but Brian felt no better. He went out into the cockpit and gurgled over the side. Once relieved, he sat back in the cockpit, as white as a sheet, took out his baccy and by moonlight rolled a cigarette to recover. I took the opportunity to make myself a quick meal. Brian did not feel like eating. I felt tired and considered the risk of sailing on without anybody on watch. Brian had taken to his bunk again and there was no point in asking how he felt, let alone if he could keep watch. Now was the time, I thought, of using the CARD (Collision Avoidance Radar Detector) and the AIS (Automatic Identification System) to sound the alarm if another ship threatened collision while I put my head down. Since we left Antigua we had not spotted a single craft or a single light, other than the solitary one on Barbuda. The ocean appeared truly deserted. I put a couple of rolls in the genoa and decided to take to my bunk, relying utterly on the adequacy of the equipment that I had now activated. *Luna Quest* sailed on unattended, guided only by the Hydrovane, the self-steering mechanism mounted on the transom. In the trade wind she would hold her course without any problem and the winds were unlikely to vary greatly from the Force Five during the night unless a squall decided to make its presence felt. *Luna Quest* sailed beautifully and gently in the regular swell and I was soon lulled into a deep sleep, not waking up until morning when daylight came pouring in through the saloon starboard windows. *Luna Quest* was still on the same compass bearing that I had set her on when retiring for the night. She clearly had not needed me or Brian and did not appear to need me now. The wind had abated to a steady Force Four from the north-east. Poking my head out of the companionway, a lovely and warming sun greeted me; the sky was blue with little white clouds sitting on the horizon. How glorious to be out on the ocean on a day like this. I hoped it might stay like this all the way home. Brian, who appeared dead to the world, missed this wonderful experience. I felt sorry that he could not enjoy this world of pure, virginal nature. He declined tea or anything to eat. He said he would soon be all right once he had found his sea legs; his body needed a little time to adjust and he declined the idea of taking any Stugeron, a seasickness tablet. He just lay in his bunk like a patient on a sickbed, curled up. He had not eaten or drunk anything since lunchtime the day before.

Luna Quest forged on, taking each wave in her stride and leaving the bow wave to rush past her, tracing the course by her wake. The world was at peace and predictable. I had promised Marion that I would be emailing her on a daily basis, weather permitting, and so after breakfast and after plotting our position, I set to work. I found it quite a joy to recall and write about our experiences. Brian kept to his bunk and did not surface other than to get up twice for a smoke in the cockpit. We were making good progress, covering 170 miles on our first day out of Antigua, no doubt aided by the North Equatorial Current. Our second night was as peaceful as the first. Brian and I slept all the way through again while *Luna Quest* did all the work without protest, without being fed and without rest. Wednesday's sunrise complemented the beauty of nature that soothed one and made one feel at one with it. The Hydrovane did not need any adjustment. The trade wind was as steady as a rock and *Luna Quest* had found a reliable partner to have her sails stroked. I loved this sailing and wanted it to go on forever. I thought how easy it was sailing to Bermuda and almost regretted the idea that we would eventually get there, make landfall and be among people again, but I knew this was a silly thought and dismissed it from my mind. We covered 150 miles the second day and Brian still had not surfaced.

Thursday gave me a thorough experience of what a squall could be like. We had seen quite a few overtaking us on the horizon on the way to St Lucia and even experienced one or two at close quarters. Whereas Tuesday and Wednesday had presented clear skies, today produced several squalls to the lee of *Luna Quest*, and one large black multi-layered one just off the starboard bow. It seemed to be growing in size as we ploughed on over the waves. Before long the entire sky was obliterated by a mass of dense low-hanging black porridge that seemed to envelop us and be bent on eating us. Suddenly, there was an indescribable pelting of cold buckets of water from above. It flattened the sea, obliterated the bow from view, filled the side-decks and half the cockpit in a matter of minutes. The scuppers and drain holes could not cope with the masses of water that almost drowned me, sitting in the cockpit wearing my oilies. The density of the rain was such that you might as well have sat in the sea. I noticed that I had difficulty taking air in and needed to keep my head down to oblige my lungs. Even in that position I found my breathing inhibited. The strength of the wind increased during this attack of nature, but not dangerously. Brian was still in his bunk, oblivious to nature's forces and of everything else around him.

When the squall had passed and the sea appeared flat around me, I began to worry about Brian. Surely, he would have noticed something! If he did not start adjusting now, he would soon lose all the physical and mental strength his slender body possessed. Perhaps it was not seasickness that he was suffering from, but some dreadful illness that he had not told me about before we set off, or that he himself had not been aware of. He was a small man of slight build, perhaps five feet, four inches tall. He had spent all his working life in the building industry as a carpenter / joiner and after his divorce had bought and restored his beloved Rhoda from a near wreck over a six-year period. On completion, when every inch had evidenced meticulous workmanship he, in the company of several experienced old salts, had sailed her over from England to St Lucia via Gibraltar and the Canaries, but here he was wasting away in the hollow of *Luna Quest* upon a solitary ocean. I had visions of him starving and dying on *Luna Quest*. Was it ten or eleven days that man could go without drinking anything before all life sapped away? How many days was it without food? Perhaps his body would not last that long. It would be at least a week to Bermuda. He would leave a daughter and a son. What would I do in those circumstances? I would have a lot of explaining to do. Looking at him, he appeared motionless, whitish grey and thinner than ever. He seemed to have shrunk as well as having lost weight. The wind fell away as suddenly as it had increased, becalming us on a flat ocean, down beaten by the rain. When the wind picked up again to around twenty-one knots, I unrolled the genny and off we sped again, unhampered by waves. I left one reef in the mainsail. Towards nightfall, the sea had assumed its former shape, but it had given Brian respite from the motion; a change had come over him. He said he felt better and would like a soft drink. It held. It made him feel hungry, which encouraged me to make a meal for the two of us, as palatable as possible. I used the best and freshest of meats and vegetables. Brian said he liked it at the first two bites, but then, suddenly, he got up and leaped into the cockpit, gurgling yet again over the side. Poor Brian was suffering ignominiously. Because he had recovered so quickly when the ocean was flattened, I felt confident that his illness was no more than protracted seasickness, which he might have overcome if he had taken the Stugeron. I suggested he took some Paracetamol, which to my surprise he accepted. They made him feel a lot better. It made me feel better as well. He would not die after all.

After washing up I turned in and slept soundly until 0445hrs when I was woken up by a full moon setting ninety degrees to port and a new sun rising ninety degrees to starboard. We were going north all right. Another beautiful day with slightly less heat in the warmth of the sun provided another confirmation that we were getting north. The stickiness in the heat had gone and life on board improved, with Brian feeling better now that the wind strength had settled to a constant sixteen knots and the boat's motion had become as easy as if we were sailing on the Blackwater River on a Sunday afternoon. Brian was up smoking in the cockpit and having cups of tea. He felt more than decidedly better and offered to do the cooking for our evening meal. A lovely chicken casserole would await me at dinner time. Our daily runs continued some 150 miles a day, taking us halfway to Bermuda. A German-flagged yacht, maybe thirty-six feet in length, crossed our bow in a north-easterly direction. I called him on the VHF. In a thick German accent its skipper advised us to avoid Bermuda since an area of deep low pressure was heading straight for it, arriving there in a few days' time, just as he had thought of making landfall in St George's harbour, Bermuda. He had therefore changed his plan and had set a new course for the Azores. A download of the weather forecast corroborated his warning, but forecasts can be wrong, and if our speed held, we might arrive before the gale did. We were concerned but not enough to turn right just yet. Flying fish kept landing on our deck and into the cockpit; the sun shone warmly; the winds were kind and Brian was off his bunk. Life was good, warm and friendly, a life that a sailor yearns for; being at one with nature, breathing in its beauty and falling asleep in its cuddly warmth while the boat that cradles him gently carries him to the home port.

However, Saturday morning bode an ill day with low hanging deep grey clouds, little wind and squalls on the horizon. It would not be long before we would be enveloped by at least one of them. The sun had vanished, the sea was flat; an eerie calm before the storm. Soon a large squall overtook us and filled the sails with twenty-eight knots of wind and tons of water from above, sending *Luna Quest* at nine knots over a smooth sea. But when the squall had passed the wind fell away to less than before its arrival. The cloud canopy stayed with us all day and by the evening it unleashed its entire contents. It rained and rained without a break for hours and hours on end, with the wind backing to the north. Brian and I were in the saloon, hunkering down in the safety of *Luna Quest*'s womb, but the sails needed to be adjusted and the Hydrovane re-set. I had to leave the safety and snugness of the saloon to do the work. In little else than my boxer shorts I went up and was deluged. Every pore was thoroughly washed out in a matter of seconds. I managed to adjust the Hydrovane and clip on the inner forestay in readiness to receive the staysail just in case the wind should pipe up, but it did not and fell away completely as the night wore on, leaving *Luna Quest* to be rolled about ignominiously by the swell. The rain had stopped now, leaving a heavy air and a sea without waves. An oily swell swayed *Luna Quest* from side to side. The pots and pans in their lockers were shunted backwards and forwards, creating an irritating din, while the swaying of the boom's traveller in its track crashed sickeningly from port to starboard, stopping me from catching any sleep. At just after midnight I could stand it no longer and restowed whatever I could to stop the deafening cacophony. I started the engine to give the boat some momentum and stability. That solved the problem. Now, on low revs, the automatic pilot switched on and the Hydrovane disabled, we turned in again and slept soundly throughout the remainder of the night.

The next day was Sunday, 6th May. St George's Harbour beckoned. Only a hundred miles to go and we would have beaten the gale. *Luna Quest* was under engine. The clouds had gone. Where was that gale that was forecast? For now it was a glorious day; the temperature very agreeable, the engine running smoothly, pushing *Luna Quest* at five-and-a-half knots towards Bermuda. We would be there in twenty hours! To celebrate the wonderful prospect we had a cooked breakfast with bacon and eggs and lots of tea. How very civilised one can be in the middle of the ocean! Later that morning white clouds appeared and spread over our area accompanied by a fine breeze from the north-east. All sail was soon hoisted and the engine shut down. What a relief to be sailing again. We checked when we might be putting into harbour and looked forward to stepping ashore again after seven days at sea. Soon the wind picked up to a Force Five over a flat sea, stirring the sea at first and later causing it to be woolly. It sent *Luna Quest* bowling along. The wind increased still further and Brian went down to his bunk, feeling unwell again. A reef was called for, but I left it for a bit as we were making such good progress. Towards nightfall dark clouds were packing in tightly on the northern horizon and seemed to be telling us 'Haste ye back'. I put a reef in the sails. The seas were building faster now than I had ever experienced before and clearly there were some bigger seas being whipped up ahead of us. We pressed on and I checked the chart. At the current rate of progress we would be making landfall in the middle of the night. I did not think that was a good idea, given that Bermuda is just a name given to a land mass of reefs that happens to be above sea level rather than below it. Most of the reefs are just below the ocean's surface and stretch for miles around the island, counting among the most treacherous in the world; thousands of wrecks are shown on the chart. The boat shuddered as though in fear of them. The wind had increased its strength considerably and the time had come for a second reef to slow her down, but having put in a second reef, she ran even faster than before. In the pitch black, I put in a third reef, hanked on the staysail and rolled up the genny. That would slow her down! But no, she kept running north at well over six knots and into an ever rising wind and sea now from the south-east. The waves had become ominously powerful with some cascading over the top of the boat, testing our hatches and windows. Sometimes *Luna Quest* would sail off a particularly steep wave, crash-landing in the hollow of the next wave and sending judders throughout the boat. Anything inside her not well secured would clatter about, adding to the tumult in the raucous din. We had to slow her down by hook or by crook or else we would be on the reefs...

The gale was now fully upon us and I suggested that maybe we should consider giving Bermuda a miss and go for the Azores. As I expressed the thought to Brian I put the boat on a course to pass Bermuda, but Brian was not keen on the idea and suggested that we hove to and wait for daylight. Brian could do with some terra firma under his feet for a while to regain his strength. We were on the wrong tack for heaving to, for on the starboard tack we would be forereaching towards Bermuda and not knowing exactly how far off we were, I judged it safer to go about and heave to on the port tack forereaching in the opposite direction. I pulled the sails in to sail as closely to the wind direction as we could. I would have to choose my moment carefully to tack among the violence of the breaking rollers, but when the moment came I found that the staysail and the third reef in the mainsail did not produce enough momentum to wear the boat around through the wind. I attempted it several times, but could not manage it. I was reluctant to attempt jibing on my own. I remembered the same experience in *Sally*, when off the east coast of England, caught out in a gale coming back from Holland. I would have to start the old Stuart Turner two-stroke petrol engine to help me through the tack. I now started *Luna Quest*'s engine and brought her around safely. She was now on the port tack with her staysail aback. The sails needed no further adjustment. We were hove to and safely forereaching at about two knots away from Bermuda.

The little ship rode the waves beautifully, as steady as a rock among the tumultuous seas, but the fury of the wind howling around us was still on the increase. Our wind speed indicator had failed. It would have shown well over fifty knots. The aggression in the waves kept all our senses on edge. The North Atlantic Passage chart that I navigated from did not link up with the large-scale chart we had on board for Bermuda and we had no electronic chart of the area either. The pilot guide warns mariners not to attempt entry into St George's Harbour in gale force winds from any easterly direction and recommends bypassing Bermuda altogether. I puzzled over how I could safely navigate off the North Atlantic Passage chart and on to the large scale chart of Bermuda without running into some outlying reef between the two. Suddenly, *Luna Quest* heeled at an awkward angle, not for long, maybe a couple of seconds, but long enough to freeze us in suspense. The sea was pressing with all its might against the little saloon windows, willing to cave them in and envelop us in its watery clutches. We could only watch in agony, hoping the windows would hold. Then the sea ran off, baring the windows and returning us to her previous list. As if this punishment wasn't enough, *Luna Quest* was now picked up by another monster, swept along and then deposited. *Luna Quest* shuddered, we shuddered, everything on the boat shuddered. I wondered if the engine was still bolted to its beds and whether the seventy-five metres of heavy-gauge anchor chain had not cracked the hull in trying to bomb through it, but all appeared intact. The rig was still up there. My God, this boat must be strong! A sense of pride came over me, but it did not linger. I began to worry about Brian being ill, about the lack of chart, about our entrance into St George's Harbour, about not being able to spot the buoy in this filthy weather and about the safety of my boat. Then a second crash! This was getting out of hand. How many more of these crashes could *Luna Quest* withstand? How much more could our nerves withstand? I called Bermuda Harbour Radio on the VHF, then on the SSB radio, not to invite their rescue services, since we were not in imminent danger of losing boat or man, but to get an idea of where this weather was going to go and to take my mind off this tumult. They answered and reassured me that the weather would have improved by the morning. I explained our position, our lack of charts and would they be able to give me a course to steer for the red-and-white safe-water buoy a mile outside the harbour entrance if I gave them my position? Yes, they could and asked me to call them first thing in the morning when the worst of the storm would have passed. They made no mention of any dangers that the pilot guide had advised mariners of. Perhaps it was not as dangerous as the pilot guide said. Perhaps the knowledge that the gale would pass allowed them to give us the confidence to make for St George's Harbour. If we had been any closer to Bermuda or if we had not hove to when we did, we could well have been blown on to Bermuda's reefs and foundered. After all, we could not have been more than fifteen, maybe twenty miles away. We would have become a statistic marked on the chart as a wreck, unnamed, unrecognised as anything but a casualty of poor seamanship. We turned in and awaited daylight. Sleep did not come easily, despite an absence of further crashes. At 0515hrs I had had enough of idling in my sleeping bag, pretending I could sleep in the din. I got up; it would be daylight soon. The wind seemed to have abated to Force Seven or Force Eight; we were no longer being thrown about so much.

To gain access to St George's Harbour, an entering vessel must negotiate a narrow channel cut through the reefs that surround the island. It is called the Cut. The land walls of it rise at ninety degrees above sea level and plunge at ninety degrees below sea level. It runs north-west / south-east, which meant that we would have the wind directly aft as we entered it. It is for good reason that the pilot guide advises mariners not to attempt negotiating this Cut when the wind is galing from anywhere in the east. But we had decided otherwise…

The weather was thick with dense and prolonged downpours, blanking out all visibility. I called Bermuda Harbour Radio and requested a course to steer. They came back with 306° True. With fifteen degrees magnetic variation shown on the chart, that would make a course to steer of 321°. The easier motion of the boat after the crashes in the hove to position had cured Brian of his seasickness and he now joined me in the cockpit. We both had our oilies on and sou'westers. We set *Luna Quest* on the adjusted course, steering by hand

and hoping for the best. The weather was truly filthy. Heavy wind and dense rain prevented us from seeing anything but water all around, below and above. At 0745hrs we made it on to our large-scale chart. With some consternation I noticed that we were nowhere near the red-and-white safe-water buoy marking the beginning of the channel that led to the Cut, but quite close to a cardinal buoy that marked the entrance into the Cut. There was no time to wonder why we had missed the red-and-white and why we had not foundered on the reefs. I checked the chart and found that we had enough water to set a new course direct for the cardinal buoy, which because of the zero visibility could not be seen, although we were less than half a mile off the coast. The density of the rain was something to be believed, but since the risk of foundering had now gone away all our concentration was focused on spotting the cardinal buoy from where it would be a jibe around it into the Cut. I put Brian on the helm to make sure he would not be sick again at this vital time while I went down below, plotting our position every five minutes on the paper chart. We were closing in and accurate navigation was called for. There was no sight of the island or the lighthouse marked on the chart. I checked and re-checked my positions. If only this dreadful rain would give us some respite! Suddenly, the rain ceased and Brian shouted that land was close to port. I bounded up the companionway and through the thick rain clouds, which seemed to touch the sea and hide the land, I could just about discern the outlines of land. Too close for comfort! It looked to me as though we were heading straight for the reefs less than quarter of a mile off the harbour entrance. Seeing land so near gave me a sudden fright and Brian great joy. We looked to be too close to the shore, despite the chart indicating that we had enough water under the keel. I took over the steering and steered my little ship by sight along the coast and away from the reefs, where huge waves were breaking thunderously in white spume. The lighthouse was now visible, a miserable looking light flashing through the rain clouds that drifted densely over the island. As expected, our course of approach demanded a gibe into the Cut. There would be no turning back once jibed. I asked Brian if he was ready for it in this make or break situation. He said he was confident that we would make it and that he wanted to go for it. His confidence gave me determination and we headed straight for the first cardinal buoy marking the beginning of the entrance.

Entrance to St. George's Harbour, Bermuda

Had Bermuda Harbour Radio given us the wrong course? Did these office boys know the difference between a cardinal buoy and a safe-water mark or had the earth's magnetism upset our compass? We were confident that we had steered the correct course. With the tiller in one hand and the mainsheet in the other I felt *Luna Quest* behaving like a dinghy racing in a big wind for the finishing line. The speed through the water was probably near *Luna Quest*'s theoretical maximum, making steering by hand a very light exercise. The slightest movement in the tiller resulted in an instant response. I prepared to jibe. The genny was furled and the staysail, fully out, would be left to its own resources. I hauled in the main sail. The moment had come. I called to Brian, "Ready to jibe," and pushed the helm to starboard and, once through the wind, I let the mainsail out to starboard. At the same time the staysail billowed out to port and like a goose in full flight we now headed straight for the Cut. As it hove into view I could not believe we would be able to sail through the tiny entrance literally cut through the reefs by the hand of man. I considered turning back, but how? The size of the waves now dead behind gave us no choice and the narrowness of the Cut convinced me that we would be shipwrecked. I rang out some expletive, but it was no use. Huge waves now lifted us up, propelling us inexorably into the Cut, assisted by the fearsome gale that held our sails as taut as a tightrope. On both sides of us furious waves were pushed up on to the reefs by the remorseless gale and pounded so that they smashed themselves into clouds of spray. I steered for the middle. The reef walls of the Cut were as tall as *Luna Quest*'s mast and I remembered in a flash a similar experience I had in *Sally* when steering into the Southwold entrance with a spring tide ebbing across. I had missed the top of the tide then by some two hours and paid for it while determinedly attempting to get in with half a gale of wind blowing from behind. In pangs of fright and anxiety, all witnessed by holiday makers standing on the sea defences high above me and waving at me in silence, I prayed I might get through, not on my knees in *Sally*'s little cockpit, but standing astride and gripping the tiller more firmly to counteract the wayward tidal stream that set me across. Then I noticed that the waters in the Cut were less tumultuous and realised that we would soon be able to keep a steadier course than when I made my Southwold entrance. Just as I had made it into the quiet waters of Southwold Harbour itself, St George's Harbour now opened up before us. We had made it. A great sense of relief and exhilaration flooded through our veins. Brian would be able to regain his strength and together we would be able to explore this paradise island as brochures will have it. Later in the week we witnessed the arrival of a big cruise ship through the Cut. Perhaps the Cut was not so small after all.

Chapter 14

Bermuda to the Azores

Although the pilot guide informs the navigator that St George's Harbour is safe in all weather conditions, which had seemed so appealing to us when we were battling the elements, the harbour did not appear to us as safe as advised. White caps flew around the harbour, tenders were blown about on their painters and one yacht was being wrenched off her anchor despite carrying no sail. She was blown downwind towards some very unyielding mass of concrete that formed the base of a magnificent building at the harbour's edge. The yacht, a lovely looking classic, appeared to be unmanned and despite our repeated efforts to alert Bermuda Harbour Radio over the VHF on Channel Sixteen of her impending doom, her drift went on inexorably to its fateful destruction. The harbour signs directed us towards a jetty where the grand building stood. No doubt, the harbour-master's office was housed on the ground floor. It is accepted convention to report to the harbour-master on arrival in any port before one ties up or lets the hook down, but the gale blew right into the U-formed harbour-master's visitors' pontoon and anybody attempting to tie up there could be certain of serious damage or loss of his ship. We motored around the harbour, looking for a place to tie up or drop the hook for the time being, but nowhere appeared safe in the gale. In the meantime we were entertained by the fate of the drifting yacht. She was now quite close to the mass of concrete. Suddenly, she stopped, turned sideways and heeled over away from the wind. She had clearly struck some underwater object that was too hard to dislodge. Because she was so close to the concrete base, she had very likely stranded on her foundations from which there was no escape. She stayed there pinned down for about fifteen minutes, heeling precariously before her owners and several crew came speeding along in the harbour-master's motor launch to deal with the situation. They waved at us gratefully. The yacht was saved.

We could not be going round and round all day until the gale had subsided and the visitors' pontoon had become safe enough to tie up. I decided to seek permission to anchor out in Convict Bay, which forms part of St George's Harbour and provides relative shelter before completing the paperwork. I called Bermuda Harbour Radio to explain my predicament and permission was granted, which was just as well as we were completely exhausted, having had little sleep and no food for quite a long time. Once anchored, we made ourselves a steaming bowl of hot porridge and took to our bunks, sinking into oblivion of the world around us. On waking up we found ourselves anchored next to Tabitha, a Rival 41, owned and sailed single-handedly by Eric Orme. He had sailed from Virginia and was ready to cross the Atlantic on his own via the Azores to Falmouth, the very route we had planned for our return. Eventually he hoped to moor her near Ramsholt in the River Deben. Some very pleasant and relaxing days were spent at anchor while our port aft lower shroud was replaced. Some of its strands had failed during the storm and if we had not put into Bermuda and carried on to the Azores, we might well have lost our mast in the next gale. The rigger expressed his surprise that the gauge of the failing shroud was only six millimetres whereas the other shrouds and stays were seven millimetres (I would be even more surprised on returning to Fox's Marina in the Orwell in December to find that all the shrouds and stays should have been eight millimetres). Tabitha set off for the Azores a week before us. For his guide and company he had registered with Herb, an elderly German weather guru living in Canada, who supplied Atlantic sailors with free routing and weather services via the SSB radio. We had not registered with him as we had our own weather services that we could download via the Iridium satellite telephone. In any case there were many conflicting reports about Herb and I did not like the idea of being told to sail to a particular location in the middle of the ocean and await further instructions.

The day before our departure, which we had reserved for taking on fresh water and fuel, brought such a fierce tropical downpour that we decided we would block up the four drain holes in the side decks (two either side) and siphon the rainwater into our water tank. Fearful that the downpour might cease as suddenly as it had started, we worked frantically to improvise stoppers. There was no time to put our oilies on, boots and sou'westers to test the stoppers in the drain holes. Stripping off was quicker. In my shorts I jumped up the companionway and out on deck to insert them in the holes. The rain was bitterly cold and pelted me so hard that I had another of nature's thorough scrubs. A few more hops up and down the companionway to adjust the size and the stoppers were ready. The volume of heavenly waters was so copious that we could have filled a second tank and probably a third if we had them. The water tasted deliciously fresh and I was grateful that I did not have to weigh anchor and make my way to the dock for taking on the island's water. A last minute dash ashore to finalise the paperwork and fresh foods purchases and we were ready for the morning departure. The dinghy was hauled on board, deflated and folded away for storage in the forecastle. Refuelling could wait until morning.

Before I flew back to Antigua to take *Luna Quest* back to England, I had seen my local doctor to have an unstable growth under the lower part of my right arm removed, just in case I knocked it whilst on passage. After she had removed it, the doctor said that I did not have to worry about it ever growing back again. Much to my great surprise, however, the growth did come back, only this time after I had returned to Antigua and in a much larger and more unstable form. It was decidedly unsightly and had become more dangerous than the first. It worried me that I was about to embark on an Atlantic crossing of some 1,800 miles with a skin growth that could present some awkward difficulties and which I thought I had got rid of. The day we set off was grey, wet and overcast with a Force Five from the north-north-east. It meant sailing close-hauled. I put a reef in the sail. Brian was seasick again. The poor devil took to his bunk from where he did not surface until after lunchtime of the following day when the wind had eased. I did not feel too great either, but forced some food down to keep reasonably energetic. Towards the early evening of that first day, I felt wetness in my right arm sleeve and, having had my oilies on all day, I wondered why it should feel so wet. I removed my oilies, jumper and shirt to investigate and was mightily shocked to see that the growth had been torn off, showing an open wound that produced copious amounts of blood. A pair of helping hands would have been ideal at that point in time to dress the wound, but Brian was out for the count and the medical stock was in the forecastle. I had to keep my arm in the air to limit the flow of blood. It would make accessing the medical supplies quite a difficult exercise. I had to climb over the sails that I keep in between the two forward bunks, but once having a firm foothold, rummaged around the medical boxes with my left arm, looking for antiseptic wipes and wound dressings. I could not use my right arm to steady myself in the pitching craft as I thought it imperative to keep that arm up in the air. Luckily, I found the First Aid kit fairly quickly. I struggled back to the saloon, dragging the kit with me where I cleaned my arm and dressed the wound as best I could in the fading light of day. I searched for the torn-off skin growth, which, after a bit of searching, I found in the bottom of my arm sleeve. The wind had now increased to Force Six and I put a second reef in to allow for less pitching during the night. From time to time *Luna Quest* would slam into some of the oncoming cross seas, sending seismic shocks through the entire frame of our little home. However, they did not prevent me from falling into a deep sleep, dreaming dreams where the slamming seemed an appropriate component of the activity dreamt. After a while the cross swell eased and the boat's motion became easier and the sleep deeper.

In the morning, Brian complained of a headache. He had not eaten or drunk anything since breakfast yesterday. As much as he was against taking any kind of medication, I persuaded him to take two Paracetamol and a glass of water. He dropped off to sleep again while the motion of the boat became decidedly easier with the cross swell tailing off further, together with the wind. By noon the sun was trying to come out through wispy clouds, giving a little brightness and warmth that had Brian up from his bunk. He proclaimed that he felt much better and that he had found his sea legs again. He rolled a cigarette, sat up on the bridge head and drank a cup of tea whilst puffing away on a joint. I gave him two slices of currant bread with honey, which perked him up no end. The wind had now disappeared altogether to make way for a new depression heading for Bermuda. We put the engine on to gain some distance from Bermuda, which seemed to lie in the track of every weather front coming off the American seaboard. It ran for the rest of the day and night, when a change in the motion of the boat woke me up at four o'clock in the morning. There was a gentle breeze from the north-east and the sky was beautifully star speckled, but no moon. I turned off the engine, set the sails and the Hydrovane and crept back into my sleeping bag. Brian had not stirred.

During the course of the day the wind blew a steady Force Four, giving us plenty of speed and a slight sea. Brian felt well again and provided a splendid salad lunch. I was glad he could eat and drink again and get some energy back into him. But the wind did not stay gentle for long and a reef was required early evening. A second reef was called for later that night. Although the sea had become a little rough, it seemed regular enough for Brian not to be seasick. He stayed up smoking his joints, watching the seas build with the freshening wind. At daybreak he turned in and stayed there without food or drink. In the afternoon it was blowing a Force Seven, but *Luna Quest* took it in her stride, sailing close-hauled under a reefed genny, staysail and reefed mainsail. Every now and again the little ship would fall off a wave and crash-land into the next, which caused a tremendous din and made her motion very uncomfortable, especially as it appeared we had a foul cross sea. Anything not tied down created the most unnerving racket, especially the jars and tins in the galley lockers. I eased her off the wind, which stopped the crashing and made the motion less violent. In the evening Brian managed to drink a small fruit juice and suck a sweet for his dinner. Having put a further couple of rolls in the genny, I took to my sleeping bag, listening to the crashing and banging inside and out. Fitful sleep came at last. In the morning the wind seemed to have eased a little, although more waves appeared to be landing in the cockpit. Despite the dancing waters around us, the Hydrovane continued to steer the ship regardless of waves, wind or speed, its leading edge always pointing into the wind thereby keeping the ship on course. The crew were hunkering down below, watching the seas speeding past, thankful that they did not have to be out in the cockpit steering the boat as their predecessors would have done half a century ago. The brave little ship seemed to thrive under the steady hand of the Hydrovane. No amount of hand-steering would have improved on that.

All day the sky was overcast with strong winds from the north-east but no rain. The temperature had now fallen to a level where I needed to wear two jumpers. What a change from Antigua where the temperature on the day we left measured forty degrees! However, the sea temperature in these higher latitudes still measured nineteen degrees Celsius. Towards the end of the day the skies cleared, giving us an opportunity to see a near perfect sunset. Brian remained in his bunk and went again without food or drink. I worried about him and hoped for a further easing of the wind. I cooked myself a steak and made a point of eating well, hoping for a better night's sleep. The wind did ease further and sleep came easily and deeply. By morning the wind had fallen to a slight breeze, but the waves remained awkward, which kept Brian in his bunk until late morning when there was insufficient wind to keep the sails filled. The mainsail slammed backwards and forwards in the swell and I decided to crank the engine into action to give the boat some stability. Brian said he felt a lot better and climbed into the cockpit to smoke his joint and enjoy his first mug of tea since the salad lunch. I lost my tea all over the saloon floor as I tried to come up the companionway to join him in the cockpit. I spent the next twenty-five minutes mopping up the tea that I had been so looking forward to. Towards the evening the seas calmed down further and under the steady motion of engine power Brian took the opportunity to cook us a much needed supper.

A tiny breeze sprang up from the south-west by midnight, just strong enough to keep the sails filled despite the gentle, rolling motion caused by the remaining swell. We enjoyed another good night's rest while our little floating home ghosted along under a moonlit sky. The lack of wind persisted throughout the day and little progress was made, but it gave Brian an opportunity to regain his former strength with lots to drink and the best of the fresh food we had shipped in Bermuda, although much of it had already perished and required to be jettisoned. During the night a light air tended from the south-south-east, which held all night and all of the following day, a beautiful summer's day, when we saw Portuguese men of war, dolphins playing across our bow and a distant explosion of a whale's exhalation sending a jet of water into the air. It was a day of sailing that even the most reluctant of sailing passengers would have enjoyed. The lack of breeze persisted, however, consistent with a slowly rising barometer. The light air stayed with us throughout the night and the next two days. There was not even enough wind to fill the light parasail or the large lightweight genny. Our progress became frustratingly slow. A little bit of motoring here and there helped us along. A school of darting multi-coloured tuna fish mocked the lazy motion of our ship. I considered that one of them would make a feast of a meal and considered how I could catch one. We were not making enough speed to trawl a line and in any case they were at the bow and not at the stern of our ship. So I thought I would try out the harpoon that I had bought in France just for this kind of occasion.

I sat for hours in the bow, waiting for the right moment. But they were too quick, never in the right position and knowingly disappeared when they thought my patience was running out and I might launch a random harpoon at them. There were at least a dozen of them. In the end my patience did run out and, having launched a couple of harpoons in vain, I gave up. At daybreak the sails were hanging limp in the rigging, not a breath of air stirred the sea. An occasional low dark cloud would lazily pass us by without shedding any rain that it might have carried. The sun shone warmly on our bodies lying prostrate in the cockpit waiting for a change, which came at noon when the barometer registered a fall of five millibars. We could be expecting wind before long. As we dozed in the cockpit we were suddenly startled by a sharp twang in the rigging, followed by a small piece of metal falling on the side deck. We were mightily puzzled, turning it over in our hands several times, peering at it and guessing where it might have come from. There was nothing for it but to climb the mast and inspect each and every fitting, but all seemed fine. We could find no clue as to its origin. The barometer continued to fall, a bit more rapidly now. In preparation of a spell of heavy weather, Brian made a supply of pancakes filled with egg, bacon and tomatoes, some drop scones with raisins and a pizza for supper.

Throughout the night the wind had been coming, gathering in strength and stirring the sea. By morning the seas were breaking, lifting and pushing our ship from the starboard quarter on a fast passage to the Azores, which now lay only 700 miles away. The south-westerly continued to gain in strength and demanded two reefs in the mainsail and half the genny. The seas began to take on the now familiar Alpine scene with the white caps being blown around reducing visibility. The rigging vibrated as our valiant little home pitched and plunged, but still the wind continued to gain in strength while the barometer continued to fall. The pizza that Brian had made the day before was not a success and we felt cheated out of a decent supper. It was too stodgy and unpalatable and we had to chuck most of it away, leaving us hungry and disinclined to try any of the other goodies he had made. The following morning we woke up to a wild scene. The ocean looked truly awesome. Huge growling waves jumped aboard, half-filling the cockpit and disappearing through the cockpit drain holes. In between the visiting growlers we padlocked the lids on the lockers in case some of them got lifted off. Two huge towers of water, steeply faced and on a converging course, hit our little cork of a boat in quick succession, one knocking her nearly over and the other slewing her around by some sixty degrees. The force of these two could have knocked her down and capsized her but for the two-second time difference in their convergence. We now feared that nature would improve on its timing of these rogue waves and we awaited the next attack. The waves that were about to break on the weather side of *Luna Quest*, but broke to leeward of her once passed, would leave a light blue frothy trail, the colour of a shallow coral sea, but if they broke to the windward side of us just before they hit the ship, they would send their tops at lightning speed smashing into the sails. An occasional monster would break over the quarter, slewing our home around by some thirty degrees and pushing the bow closer to the wind, causing the sails to flog and the rigging to shake, but the Hydrovane would always bring her back on course. We should have put the third reef in, but we were hoping for the wind to ease. The prospect of going on deck in these awesome conditions was truly forbidding and we kept putting it off...

Our CARD picked up a radar signal on our starboard side and sounded the alarm. Of course, we could not see anything through the saloon portholes in the general tumult of nature's forces, but it was an opportunity to divert the mind from an existing fear to a new and more focused exercise. I called the vessel on the VHF and, much to my surprise, got an answer. They were in the middle of taking all their sails in bar a scrap on the forestay. She was a two-masted seventy-two-footer, professionally skippered and heading for Horta in the Azores. They reported wind speeds of over fifty knots and were surprised to learn that we had not reefed down to the minimum yet. A French forty-three-foot Ovni yacht, who picked up our radio contact, called us from our port side. They, too, were heading for Horta. By early evening the wind began to whistle, giving off an ominous ring. It rained off and on without any let up in the weather. Before the evening got too dark, we decided to take in the last reef. Brian had not been feeling too well and had not risen from his bunk since the wind had got up, but to do the job I needed an extra pair of hands. We talked through the procedure, revised it and went through the details again. There was no room for error. We donned our wet gear, strapped on our safety harnesses and hooked on to the jacklines that ran all the way around the boat over the side decks from fore to aft. I dislike using them as they can be a dangerous hindrance when doing a simple job on deck, but needs must as in the current conditions the risk of being washed overboard was considerable. Gingerly, I ventured forward to the mast on the starboard side to release the main halyard and pull the sail down while Brian crept up on the port side, armed with the winch handle. The mast did not have a reef handle pocket, so Brian had to hold on to it while I dealt with the reefing. The sail came down remarkably easily despite the pressure of the wind in the sail. In fact, the entire operation had not been anywhere near as dangerous as feared. Returning to the cockpit, I was overtaken by a massive wave that came cascading from the direction of the bow down the side deck, swamping me off my feet and filling my boots with warm seawater. There was something pleasurable and comforting about the deluge of water that enveloped me, but I had a good hold and the wave continued to wash down the boat's side decks without me. In the cockpit we furled the genny to a mere third of its full size, which eased the pressure on the rigging and boat considerably. The boat's motion had now become easier, taking the speed down to seven-and-a-half knots.

Brian crept back into his bunk, feeling utterly miserable, refusing all food and drink. I cooked myself some rice and chilli con carne from a packet on a dancing stove and hoped the weather would ease soon. As I ate my food, I noticed from the GPS that we were no longer heading for Horta, but for the Canaries. It meant that the wind had swung to the west and that we would have to jibe before long to put us back on our course. I deliberated whether to get Brian up to help me gibe the boat, deciding in the end that an extra pair of hands would be useful. It was raining hard and we needed to put our wet gear on again. I found my boots completely soggy and knew they would never dry out unless they were rinsed out in fresh water and left in the sun for a day. Brian's gear was reasonably dry. We struggled into our protective clothing on a slippery and jumping floor of the saloon. I wondered whether putting my boots on would serve any purpose, but decided to do so in any case if it was just to protect my feet in case I slipped whilst carrying out the jibe. At last we were ready and climbed into the cockpit, like two caricatures in heavy and cumbersome protective clothing, squeezing through the companionway opening. The jibe was effected without incident; a new course was set and the Hydrovane adjusted. Luckily, there were no furious waves shooting across the boat while we were carrying out the manoeuvre. We got back into the saloon unharmed. *Luna Quest* surged on regardless, controlled utterly by the Hydrovane.

Not long afterwards, the rain stopped and the wind seemed to ease, but the boat's motion was still quite bad, making Brian horribly sick. I feared for the building of nasty cross seas with a further veering of the wind and a worsening motion of the boat that would have Brian in his bunk for a lot longer. I did not say anything and hoped for the best. I was in the process of making myself a cup of tea to consider the current state of affairs when a sudden lurch lifted me off my feet and sent me flying across the saloon. I had an open milk carton in my hand at the time, which inevitably lost much of its contents over the chart and papers on the chart table and, how I cannot say, on the ceiling. I spent the next thirty minutes sliding across the saloon floor, clearing up the mess, and feeling utterly exhausted by having to stabilise myself whilst carrying out the task. By two o'clock in the morning I crawled into my sleeping bag among the din of clattering and rolling of anything and everything that was not screwed or bolted down. Despite the din, sleep came easily, helped by an easing of the wind. It was now 1st June, 2007 which gave us hope for better weather. The gale was over, but it left an overcast day and a heavy swell with all of its aggressive energy dissipated.

The gale had exacted its toll all right, a toll that we would not be able to pay again should we have another gale now. Apart from our exhaustion, I noticed that the 7mm starboard lower shroud showed unravelling strands and that the tricolour light had packed up, probably shaken senseless. There was nought we could do about the shroud and hoped it would hold until we got to Horta, only 300 miles away, where we could have it replaced. As soon as the sea was calm enough, I tried to climb the mast to bring down the tricolour light for repairs, but got not much further than just above the hounds when I realised that the swell would not allow me any let-up in my two-handed grip of the mast, so that if I managed to get to the top of the mast, I would not be able to take the tricolour light off. I came down feeling thoroughly whacked after fifteen minutes of countering the swaying of the mast. We would have to do without the tricolour light.

The gentle weather and lazy swell made us heavy with sleep, and whilst the cockpit seats were not really long enough to stretch out fully for a good rest, they proved more than adequate for our weary bodies. The feared veering of the wind to a strong north-westerly associated with a cold front never materialised. All day and night we enjoyed delightful sailing, but in the morning we found that whilst we had been fast asleep throughout the entire night, which had become our normal routine, the Hydrovane had followed the wind round from a westerly direction to the north-east. That, unfortunately, is the only downside of leaving the boat to be guided by the Hydrovane; it keeps the boat dead on course in relation to the wind direction. If the wind changes direction, then the boat changes with it. It was the first time that this had happened to me unnoticed and I felt a little stupid about it, but the day was beautiful; a cloudless sky and a warm sun made us soon forget our navigational lapse of attention. Unfortunately, the new gentle wind was now directly from the very direction we wanted to go. After first trying the port tack and then the starboard tack, we settled for the port tack as that seemed to give us the least loss of height as measured against our course to Horta in the Azores, but the wind remained frustratingly gentle and our desire to get home had taken on an energy of its own. We had sixty hours of fuel left or 300 miles and decided to use some of it in the hope of finding a better wind further north-east. After six hours of relentless motoring into the breeze, we found that the wind had veered just south of east. It was enough to lay a new course for sailing. Relieved the engine was stopped, we fretted over our slow progress, but our fretting would soon swell to anxiety as the sky overcast in the afternoon bringing drizzle and low dark clouds.

The fishing line sounded the alarm. The rod bent over, straining under great tension. It looked as though we might have caught something big at last. We leapt up and were very excited to see some hundred yards astern an even greater excitement. A flock of shearwater birds that seemed to have come from nowhere in very little time now concentrated on the one spot where our line seemed to end, crying, sweeping and diving. What was going on? We started to haul in the line. It felt heavy. As long as the fish swam in the same direction as our boat the hauling in was quick and easy, but if it went off into another direction, it became almost impossible and the hauling in had to stop. There was such great commotion among the birds and so many more shearwaters had come to flap around our prey that we could not tell what it was we had caught. The winding in became heavier and heavier the nearer it came to the boat and the moments of no tension became almost non-existent. The fish clearly feared he would be demolished soon! Then we noticed that, instead of a fish at the end of the line, there was a shearwater bird, flapping wildly in the water and ducking under from time to time. It was clearly in huge distress, as were its friends in the air. Every time it ducked, its out-spread wings transformed the bird into a kind of sea-anchor. We carried on hauling it in, gently but firmly, then clamped our hands around its wings and body and brought it into the cockpit. We had some difficulty controlling this amazingly strong bundle of energy. Our hook had pierced one of its webbed feet, which appeared like thick tough rubber. The hook had not damaged the webbing at all, despite the fierce struggle the bird had offered. Whilst Brian held the bird I tried to dislodge the hook, but the webbing was so tough that I could not work the hook back through the same hole. It would not tear either. I was considering using my marlin spike to enlarge the hole as an alternative to just cutting the line and leaving the hook in the webbing for ever, when the bird suddenly clamped its beak around Brian's index finger. Brian squealed and thought he was going to lose it, so strong was the vice-like grip. The bird's upper and lower beaks had little teeth all round like a fine double saw. Brian pleaded to get the hook out as fast as possible. I gave it my all and succeeded in wrenching it out. Brian threw it over the side, where it flopped into the sea, exhausted but relieved. After about fifteen seconds it had regained its strength and composure and flew off. Brian shook his hand to dissipate the pain. Luckily, the bird's little teeth had not been long enough or apart enough to penetrate the skin, but they had left a nasty red bruising mark.

Only another 120 miles to Horta… We could be arriving some time tomorrow, but our excitement was dampened by the persistent drizzle, the poor visibility and the light winds from the wrong direction, i.e. the east. We put the radar on in case there was any coastal traffic about and set the alarm. We also turned the VHF on to pick up any coastal maritime messages; there might even be a weather forecast in Spanish. The rain persisted into the morning, by which time the seas had assumed a nasty, lumpy behaviour that slowed us down even more. We employed some engine power to keep the speed up and hoped the weather would not deteriorate. Later that morning the easterly wind rose to a Force Five, slowing us even more. This did not bode well for making landfall. We had the wind, the current and the waves against us and were becoming anxious that we might have to stay out another night before making landfall. Then, out of the blue, we were called on the radio: the skipper of the seventy-two-footer, who had called us in the mid-Atlantic gale, came on to warn us of an impending gale in the afternoon and that we should make all haste to get into Horta. The skipper had evidently estimated our time of arrival and from the comfort of Horta harbour, where he was already moored up, had thought of our predicament. Brian and I were suddenly galvanised into action. It was a question of either getting into Horta before the gale unleashed or being tossed about for at least another night and a day, maybe longer. We increased the revs as much as we dared, shook a reef out and went hell for leather, close-hauled. Within half an hour the easterly wind had increased to a Force Six and we were obliged to put the reef back in again. Heavy rain shielded any sight of the island group. We ploughed on into the lumpy sea, spray being whipped up both sides of our bow. We struggled to make three knots. When a lull appeared in the rain we could see the peaks of some of the islands. We headed for the lee of the island, hoping for less lumpiness in the waves. As we were creeping towards the island, the wind increased yet again in strength and the rain became heavier, blanking out any visibility we had. Our speed dropped to two knots.

From the VHF we knew that our French friends in the Ovni were to the north of us and having the same awful weather, but a better point of sail. They, too, were extracting every available knot from their boat. As we got closer to the land, the rain suddenly ceased for a few minutes, just as it had when we were almost upon the reefs of Bermuda, giving us a spectacular sight of the rocks that we were now heading for. Distances are deceptive, but we were less than half a mile away. Suddenly, the waves were less pugnacious and our speed increased in the lee of the island, helped by a little headland that projected half a mile further up the coast, but the wind had now reached Force Seven and it seemed that the pelting rain had become even stronger and heavier. We were afraid that, once we had cleared the little headland, we would be mauled by the fangs of wind, sea and spray; we would be set back despite full throttle. I discussed with Brian the option of tacking out, first on the port tack and then back in on the starboard tack, making the distance to Horta harbour twice as long, but making landfall before dark still a probability. Brian thought we should persist in our present strategy and hold on. I was grateful for not having wasted our fuel on windless days when under engine we would have made more progress than under sail. On the other hand, if we had kept motoring on those windless days, we would now have been inside the harbour of Horta, all tied up, cosy and safe. The time had come to use it up and under full throttle. With heavy hearts we inched around the headland into the fury of wind and sea. The harbour entrance was now in view in between the heavy bouts of rain and as luck would have it another headland beyond the harbour further east gave us just enough protection from the wildest waves to maintain an average speed of one-and-a-half knots. We were thrown back frequently but felt confident we would make it, provided the engine did not fail; we held on like dogs holding on to their bone. Fuming spray was flying past us at supersonic speed. One was in real danger of doing oneself serious damage to the eyes if one attempted to look ahead outside the protection of the spray hood. Another half-hour of this gruelling test and we would be in. At last we could make our entrance. No sooner were we inside the harbour than the full gale unleashed itself, tossing about the boats at anchor in the harbour. I did not fancy joining them and kept motoring around just as I had done in St George's Harbour in Bermuda, until I decided to raft up alongside another boat already rafted up alongside a smaller boat at the fuel pontoon. They would not be going anywhere in this weather, giving us some peace for the time being.

The Caribbean

PART 5
A DARK RETURN

Chapter 15

Horta

I do not remember which was worse, the gale howling around the harbour or *Luna Quest* threatening to mount the boat she was supposed to be tied up to. The three boats tied to one another, with the one on the inside also tied to the fuel jetty, had great difficulty staying tied down and together. Each had her own idiosyncratic bounce on the wild waves in the harbour, putting a particular strain on the ropes that tied them together. Whilst I was tending to the ropes and managing the fenders, the harbour-master came out of his office, saying that we could not tie up at the fuel jetty and commanded us to anchor out in the harbour. Easier said than done, but we obliged, cast off and went around the harbour yet again, looking for a spot. Boats were wildly pitching and gyrating on their anchors with nobody in sight on any of them. If any crew had been on board, they were probably hunkering down in their saloons, partaking of the strong stuff to calm their nerves. There was nowhere safe with enough room to cast the anchor. I decided to attempt the marina. It seemed an ideal spot, right upwind, sheltered from wind and sea, with ready access to all the town's facilities. It would of course be full, but you cannot tell unless you try. We motored gently towards the entrance in full view of the harbour-master's office, which was strategically placed near the entrance and the fuel jetty. He must have seen us making our approach for he came out of his office, waving his arms furiously: "Anchor, anchor!" he commanded yet again and disappeared back into his office before he got too wet or windswept. Anchoring, I knew, was not an option for us and the harbour-master could not possibly judge that there was any space for anchoring as he was more concerned about stopping boats from entering the marina and keeping himself dry in the office than directing newcomers to a safe place to tie up. I decided that the least dangerous place was the fuel pontoon, whether the harbour-master liked it or not. It was not as though there was a queue of boats wanting to shelter from the gale. *Luna Quest* and the Ovni were the only two boats seeking refuge. I went up to the fuel jetty and parked *Luna Quest* as best I could alongside the second yacht rafted up. She was a French steel yacht with a forbidding rubbing strake, which, because she was so much larger and higher than *Luna Quest*, could do some serious damage, but there was nothing else for it. I knew I would be inviting the harbour-master's invective and just as I had begun to tie up, he came out again: "Anchor, anchor," he shouted at us. He said something else as well, but his words were lost in the Spanish wind as he made his way back to the office. I ignored him and carried on tying up. I needed to employ all my fenders at different heights to minimise the risk of damage. Another boat rafted up elsewhere was reported to have been squeezed between two larger boats and damaged.

"Don't you respect what I say?" was the first thing he said when I walked into his office to report my arrival and complete the paperwork. I explained that I had a broken shroud and that I needed a quiet spot to effect repairs and asked him if there were a possibility to go into the marina. He looked at me as though I was Mr Cheek from Hell. He said emphatically, "No, no place in marina," and that was that and told me again to go out and anchor. "How long you stay?" I said we would leave as soon as the shroud was mended and the weather had improved. He said I could stay where I was until the morning when the fuel jetty had to be cleared. Both the marina and harbour were chock-a-block with yachts all waiting for the weather to improve before continuing their voyage north, but for now the gale was forecast to develop into a storm later. As a result I could not see any urgency in moving off the fuel jetty. Who would want to fuel up in the gale or set off in the storm? All night long the ropes strained, screeched and pinged. Because of the French boat's nasty sharp-edged aluminium rubbing strake, I worried that *Luna Quest* would sooner or later bash into the underside of it by force of a lifting wave. There was little peace and less sleep. I went out several times in the night to check the fenders. They looked on the point of bursting, but they held. The weather continued abysmal. What would it be like tomorrow if the gale would develop into a storm? The following morning brought the onset of typical cold front weather with heavy showers. All day people talked about the storm and spent their time preparing for the worst. I took a walk around the marina and found two unused parking slots. I had also noticed that another Rival called Tabitha was rafted up in the marina in a row of four boats, whereas other rafts of boats counted five. If *Luna Quest* could be the fifth boat next to Tabitha, the last place for rafting up would have been used. Determined to avail myself of a better spot, I walked into the harbour-master's office, sat down opposite him and challenged him on the empty slots. He said he could not let me have the parking slots in the marina itself as they belonged to owners who might return at any time (as though they would in the storm), but, he said, if the owner of Tabitha allowed me to raft up to his boat, then I had his permission. As I knew Tabitha from Bermuda, the owner definitely wouldn't deny me tying *Luna Quest* to his boat. If anything, he would probably welcome us before somebody else spotted the slot. In less than half an hour we were next to Tabitha, enjoying the relatively sheltered conditions of the over-occupied marina.

In anticipation of the storm, the harbour authorities had called on each boat in the marina, requesting each one to cast out an anchor as additional holding security, i.e. additional to being tied up to the finger pontoons. All afternoon, owners were busy re-tying their boats and casting anchors. By evening every boat was so well secured that the marina and its boats had made one solid mass, with hundreds of lines criss-crossing. I suppose it must have been the density of the field of boats, masts and rigging, all tied together into one mass; one entity that the storm's savage force now took control of. As the marina appeared to be a relatively recent addition within the large brick harbour walls, probably as its size no longer warranted saving the space for the former mail boats from the Americas, now the entire marina the storm dislodged from within the harbour walls, pushing it towards the harbour entrance out to sea. Every available man in the middle of the night was called upon to arrest the break-away marina, tying it to the land with double chains, straps and ropes. Anything and everything on land that could be used to tie the marina to was used, even lamp posts, trees and benches in the pavements were used to tie the marina to, and all that in a storm where you could not stand straight. If the marina had not been secured in the nick of time, *Luna Quest*, as the last boat in the marina and nearest to the entrance, would have been the first boat to be demolished under the weight of the runaway marina. I dread to think how narrowly we escaped disaster…

Once we had fitted the new shroud, we were eager to find a gap in the weather to set off on our last lap to Falmouth. There was another area of low pressure on the way and another one after that. We could not wait forever and prepared to set off. A few more boats had made the same decision and perhaps it was a good thing because new arrivals were bound to want a place in Horta to rest after enduring the violent storm. Tabitha and *Luna Quest* sailed off together on Saturday morning, 9th June, 2007, but in the evening Tabitha came on the VHF to tell us that Herb Hilgenberg, the Canadian weather guru, had advised against making any further progress and to divert to Terceira to shelter from the next gale. The sky had already taken on an ominous look, with black clouds starting to cover the otherwise blue sky. The good strong wind had disappeared to make way for a fickle and indecisive little baby sister light air, the calm before the storm. Terceira was only some fifty miles to the south-east and we ardently hoped that we would make landfall before the new gale was upon us. We did our utmost to make all speed and this time providence was with us because we reached the marina in Terceira at about 0630hrs on Sunday without incident. There we stayed for an entire week, sheltering from one gale after another. It was just as well as we had time to repair the cooker that had developed a malfunctioning second burner. We had been prepared to set off with one functioning burner only.

Chapter 16

A windy passage

On Saturday, 16th June at 1630hrs, Tabitha, Fai Tira, a steel forty-three-foot Bruce Roberts twin-masted ketch, which had also sought shelter in Terceira, and *Luna Quest* prepared to set off for England. Whereas Tabitha, moored next to *Luna Quest* in the marina, was able to turn out of its tight slot into the wind under full thrust with the rudder hard down, we did not have enough thrust in our folding propeller to do the same. However many times we tried, the Force Five wind would not let us turn the vessel in the marina and eventually managed to blow us down to the bottom of the marina, where we came to rest, pinned down by the wind, alongside a moored motor yacht, whose owner seemed to be absent at the time. Now there was no way we could free ourselves without the help of many hands and a tow. Luckily, the harbour-master had been able to commandeer a small boat as its own launch was in for repairs. The small boat he and his mate steered towards us appeared very small indeed. It had the tiniest outboard engine on its stern. I feared that it would not have enough power to haul us off into a Force Five wind. Once made fast and the outboard revved up, clouds of blue smoke billowed from the stern, blown straight downwind into the faces of *Luna Quest*'s crew. *Luna Quest* began to move and, with the help of a few willing hands, she moved off the motor yacht and obediently pointed her bow at the blue smoke. We were now under our own power and we thanked the harbour-master for his kindness. Once outside in the open sea, we could see Tabitha in the distance, making straight for the northern horizon. Fai Tira was no longer to be seen.

We hoisted the sails, put a reef in the main, set the Hydrovane and soon we were catching up with Tabitha. We held conference. Her skipper worried about the weather and wanted to await Herb's advice that was scheduled to be received at 2030hrs. The gale and the area of low pressure that we had managed to avoid was now intensifying in the Western Approaches, well to the north of us, and waiting to join up with another area of low pressure to the west of Ireland. If we headed home now there was a real danger that we might sail into a double deep depression, with all its consequences. We agreed to hang around and await Herb's advice. To kill time and gain height into the westerly wind, which had now increased to Force Six, we headed north-west, sailing close-hauled and bashing into the windy weather. It was uncomfortable to say the least. Brian was back on his bunk. Tabitha called us later in the evening. Herb's advice was not to proceed any further north. After some deliberation, we all agreed to heave to and await events on Monday. Monday came grey, windy and rainy. Another conference was held and more uncertainty ensued. Later in the morning Brian and I decided that despite Tabitha's intention to wait yet another day for Herb, we would not and set off east to get under the depression so that we might head north later. While the wind had now increased to Force Seven, the depression could not stay where it was forever, and would eventually track north-east over the European Continent, dissipating as it left the Western Approaches. The motion of the boat became instantly pleasant with the Force Seven westerly air stream now blowing from behind. If the intensifying and now enlarged area of low pressure remained stationary for longer than expected, we now contemplated giving up heading for Falmouth altogether and going for the Mediterranean instead. It would be an easy sail and we would be there in a few days. It was a very tempting Plan B. As it was we were making cracking progress east.

In the evening a French yacht scudded past under low clouds and driving rain, heading for La Rochelle, and at the same time for the centre of the low pressure area. We wished him well on the VHF. The weather was still rough on Tuesday and Tabitha decided to wait another day for Herb's advice as did Fai Tira, but the crew of *Luna Quest* consulted their own sources of weather information and ignored any further advice from Herb that Tabitha relied on. I suggested to Brian that we should not risk losing the benefit of the area of low pressure or risk being overtaken by the high pressure ridge that was pushing with all its might against the low pressure area, creating potentially storm conditions. I further suggested that if we made north now we might ride the strong breeze all the way home, especially once the enlarged area of low pressure started to track north-east, which in the final analysis it was bound to do and fill. Brian agreed and we broke rank, said our farewells and headed north, bound for Cornwall. Tabitha and Fai Tira remained hove to for another three days as advised by Herb, but on Tuesday, 19th June at noon, we were on our way in rough seas under an ominous overcast sky. I now regretted having made so much easting as it meant having to sail closer to the direction of the strong westerly to north-westerly wind. Brian took his seasick tablets as planned and was mightily surprised that he suffered no ill effects. On the contrary, he felt remarkably well. He actually enjoyed the sailing and now regretted not having taken the tablets earlier on in the voyage. We downloaded our weather grib files regularly and became more worried about losing the benefit of the area of low pressure than running towards its centre, for the weather systems were on the move at last. Our passage was rough, though. Our little ship pitched and crashed from wave to wave, some washing right over her and along the ship's decks. If anything, the seas might get a lot worse, because the centre of the depression would have left nasty, turbulent water behind with cross swells from a veering wind. Sometimes a sudden lurch would develop into a resounding crash after *Luna Quest* had scaled some monumentally high wave, smashing down its back into the next oncoming wave as though it were a load of bricks crashing and pulverising from the scaffolding boards into a cloud of dust spray. But despite having three reefs in the main sail and the genny half out, our progress was fast.

The wind was now backing to the south-west, which gave us an easier and faster point of sail. It meant that the depression was not moving east, but north, perhaps even slightly north-west. The sea state did not improve with it and became confused and threatening, despite the wind easing to Force Five, but that did not appear to be a problem for the dolphins that played around the bow for long periods of time. A whale's spout was spotted not far off. Cooking was difficult and whatever we could produce we were forced to eat from the dog bowls that I had shipped just for these occasions. A great many valuables peas and potatoes went missing from their receptacle during preparation and eating. What did Herb know that we did not? We were getting on towards the Western

Approaches with the weather conditions seemingly deteriorating, although the wind strength had diminished. The sky continued to be littered with dark grey clouds, rain from time to time, and it had become distinctly cold. Because of the change in wind direction, the point of sail had become easier and had allowed us to push the little boat as fast as we could under full genny and three reefs in the mainsail. She appeared to like that rig now that the wind was blowing just abaft the port beam at between seventeen and twenty-four knots.

Suddenly, much to our surprise, a trawler with its arms outspread was headed straight for us at great speed. In a mass of spray it seemed bent on going for us. The situation beggared belief. There was no time to get on the radio and ask them politely for their intentions. I jumped to the tiller, overrode the Hydrovane and bore away just in time to avoid collision. We waved at the men on the trawler that pitched and rolled on a reciprocal course, never showing any sign of an apology. They waved back at us as though they had not been aware of the impending calamity. Then, to our even greater surprise, there was a second trawler with outspread derricks, running equally fast and also heading straight for us, although we had already borne away quite a bit from our original course to avoid the first. I could not bear off much more for fear of inviting a jibe, so I kept the boat headed on the same course, preparing mentally to bear off at the last minute. We did exactly that and avoided a second collision. Then I heard voices on the radio in foreign gobbledegook. The trawlers were clearly together and perhaps had had no more ill intent than simply wishing to satisfy their curiosity to see who these mad yachtsmen were, or at worst scaring us. If that had been the case, they had certainly succeeded. Because the weather was so miserable, with reduced visibility and the night nearly upon us, we activated the radar and turned the CARD off. This required around the clock screen watching and keeping a good look-out as best we could at any rate in the murk. Radio contact with Tabitha and Fai Tira reported that they were now becalmed and were motoring under a hot sun hundreds of miles to our south. The ridge of high pressure had clearly overtaken them.

Our passage continued cold and dark, with occasional rain for the next few days. I had two thermals on, two jumpers, my ski jacket and salopettes. I felt like a Michelin man, round and cumbersome, but the cold was deeply penetrating, although in reality the temperature was probably not less than sixteen degrees centigrade. The area of low pressure was clearly on the move and probably filling as the wind had lost much of its punch, but the low overcast sky continued to hold us in sombre mood, not helped by the radio receipt of a fresh gale warning over Ireland; just our luck. We were only a day or so away now from Cornwall and were very likely to be very close to either escaping it or being caught out in it. We were still making reasonable progress as nightfall came. Our radar was off, but our CARD was back on again. Suddenly, it went berserk, sending alarm signals from every quadrant rather than just the quadrant where radar would indicate its target. For a moment we feared we were surrounded by the Royal Navy or perhaps a foreign one. We peered and peered into the murk, willing to see lots of ships, but there was nothing. *Luna Quest* sailed on undisturbed and regardless of our fears. Thinking the gadget had developed a malfunction, we switched it off and peace returned. Then, dead ahead of us on our very course, an unlit grey hulk of a large ship and what later looked like a Navy Destroyer loomed up out of the murk. With the help of the binoculars we could discern a lit-up helipad on the stern with a helicopter parked on it. We decided that it must be the coastguard checking on who was coming into or leaving the Western Approaches. We now speculated that we might be boarded and searched, wasting valuable passage time if we wanted to get into Falmouth before the gale arrived. We kept our course, heading straight for the hulk. It was our right of way. For a time it kept stationary, but seeing that we were applying the collision regulations as the stand-on vessel, they moved off slowly, very slowly and then disappeared into the murk. We thanked our blessings.

We were now eager to make Falmouth as soon as possible. We were over the continental shelf, which we could tell by the fairly sudden change in colour the sea had taken, less blue and perhaps a tinge of green. It had also lost its long deep swell while more and more craft were encountered, particularly trawlers and other fishing craft. It gave us a warm feeling of getting back in home waters, and it looked as though we might reach Falmouth by the next night if the wind held, or else the following morning, Monday, 25th June. But the wind began to lose any strength it had until it failed altogether, probably in deference to the building of the new area of low pressure over Ireland that was coming our way. We put the engine on and tried to outrun the onset of the new gale, maintaining a speed of at least five knots. Getting to Falmouth by Sunday evening began to look less promising. A sailing boat under power is not anywhere near as fast or powerful as one under sail. All night we carried on under power on a calm sea, but the following morning, Sunday, a new Force Four breeze sprang up from the west, giving us a boost to our speed. Instead of the five knots under power alone we were now running at seven knots with the wind on the quarter, but I calculated that even with this speed we would not be making Falmouth until Monday morning. Falmouth Coastguard updated its gale warning at 2115hrs for sea areas Plymouth and Portland. At 2142hrs it issued a gale warning for sea areas Fastnet and Lundy, arriving 'soon' (i.e. in six hours' time). That meant the gale would be upon us in the early hours of Monday morning, when we could expect to be between the Scilly Isles and Cornwall. We discussed the option of running into Newlyn, a fishing port not, it is reported, usually friendly to yachts. We called Falmouth Coastguard on the VHF to seek their advice, but they could not tell us whether Newlyn had any space to give shelter to a yacht. So we ran on while the sky took on the foulest of appearances I have ever seen. The low clouds were literally black, stacked by dark grey ones and moving around one another ominously, yet not producing much more than a Force Four at sea level, but no rain, not for the moment at least. It would not be long, though. We knew we were in for a blow and prepared ourselves mentally. We switched on the electronic plotter to help us navigate in case it became too rough to use paper charts. Perhaps this was the gale that Herb had had in mind when he advised Tabitha and Fai Tira not to proceed to England. It seemed a long shot to have predicted this gale a week in advance, so we put it down to our own misfortune that seemed to have a nasty habit of pursuing us every time we put into port. First when putting into Bermuda, then into Horta and now into Falmouth. We prayed and hoped we would not be hit and be cast off into the English Channel.

To be in a gale in the English Channel cannot be much fun. The sea would be short and steep with plenty of venom in the waves. Low clouds or heavy rain would obscure visibility in one of the busiest waters in the world. There would not be the sea room to heave to and go to sleep. We passed Land's End, then the Lizard, and still no evidence of the gale that should have been upon us at 0300hrs, whereas now it was 0800hrs. We admired the ruggedness of the Cornish coast, the beautiful green fields and the multi-coloured natural granite sea defences. At last the Manacles hove into view. Another hour and we would be in, tucked up and safe in the marina. Our misfortune, however, caught up with us, because no sooner had we rounded the Manacles cardinal buoy to sail up to Falmouth in the River Fal, than the gale unleashed its fury like a gunshot. Luckily, we were around the headland and in protected waters, but the gale laid our little home over to starboard at an ominous angle and gave her such an instant momentum that I feared our speed would be taking us uncontrollably into anything in our path towards the Fal River. We hastily reefed the genny. The mainsail was already down to its last reef in anticipation. Then the heavens opened and deluged us with such intense and dense rain and hail that I could hardly see the bow of my ship as it raced in the general direction of the Fal. Brian was on the chart plotter, giving me directions. I thanked modern technology for giving us such gadgets, for the weather had completely blanked out visibility of all the various obstacles I had seen on our way around the buoy and up to the Fal, but I had taken good note of the positions of any traffic and was reasonably confident that the path we were coursing along was clear. Just as we were about to enter the river, the rain ceased as abruptly as it had started. The skies cleared, but the gale stayed. Once in the river, we dropped the sails and put the engine on, which, at near full throttle, just managed to hold the boat headed into the teeth of the gale. At the slightest abatement, *Luna Quest* was able to edge a little forward. Eventually, we were able to turn left and, having the gale now on the starboard side, *Luna Quest* made rapid progress toward Falmouth marina. We forgot about the gale and tied up with the help of many hands.

Having completed an Atlantic Circuit, *Luna Quest* nearly came to grief in Falmouth marina, where local workmen, whom I had requested to carry out some maintenance work while I went home in Essex, had used the heads for personal convenience without turning the sea cocks off properly. The loo flooded and spilled the waters from the Fal into our little home, unnoticed and without anything to stop it until later in the week, when a workman returned to find *Luna Quest* with eleven inches of water standing in the boat.

Epilogue

On a hasty return to *Luna Quest* I was met by an extremely sorry sight of the devastation that the water ingress had caused. She sat hauled out in the local yard with her seacocks removed, dripping. The yard denied all responsibility and advised me to lodge an insurance claim. I made a list of the damage and rang my insurance company. Much to my surprise and on the advice of a local loss adjuster, the claim was met in full excluding personal possessions, such as tools, charts and any locker contents. The yard had nearly 5 months' work.

In December of 2007 on completion of the repair works, Eric Orme and I set off from Falmouth to sail *Luna Quest* back to my home waters on the river Orwell. An area of high pressure had ensured we had bitter head winds for the entire week it took to get back, aided by much engine power and sailing overnight only twice. We ran out of fuel outside Dover harbour with ferries crossing us left and right and Eric down in the engine compartment trying to change the fuel filter, but in the end we made it to Fox's Marina, just below the Orwell bridge, where I visit her from time to time and take her out on the river on a nice sunny Sunday afternoon.

THE END

APPENDIX

RIVAL 38A CUTTER
BLUEPRINTS

7

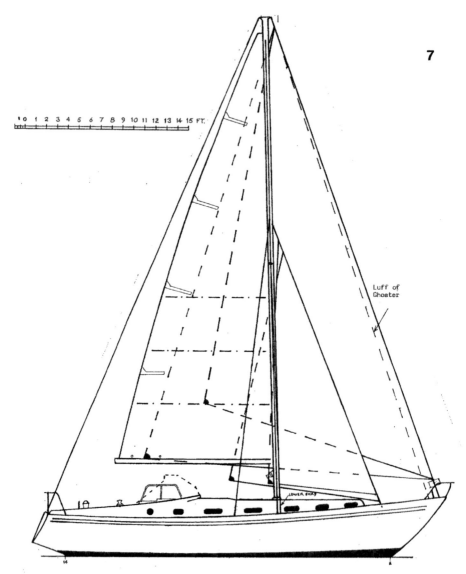

Luff of
Ghoster

SAIL SPECIFICATION

	WEIGHT OZ.UK	LUFF	FOOT	LEACH	PERP^r	AREA S.F.	NOTES
MAINSAIL	10	37' 9"	13' 9"	39' 0"	13.75	260+22 roach	Taped luff; 10" roach; 5½" h'bd; battens 26" & 29"; 3 slab reefs each 4'9" deep.
ROLLER YANKEE	8	43' 0"	21' 9"	34' 0"	17.0	365	Luff to suit roller.
GHOSTER	2½(Dy)	43' 3"	25' 7"	40' 3"	24.3	502	Rope luff and bronze hanks.
STAYSAIL	8	24' 0"	14' 0"	21' 0"	12.2	146	Wire luff and bronze hanks.
STORM STAYSAIL	10	26' 0"	11' 0"	19' 6"	7.7	100	ditto ditto
SPINNAKER	1½(Dy)	43' 5"	25' 9" width	43' 5"		1000 approx	Luff and leach in different colours.

RIVAL 38A   CUTTER WITH ROLLER JIB

PETER BRETT ENTERPRISES LIMITED   No 310/ 49B   DATE: 29.5.81
The Pitts, Bonchurch, Ventnor, I.W.

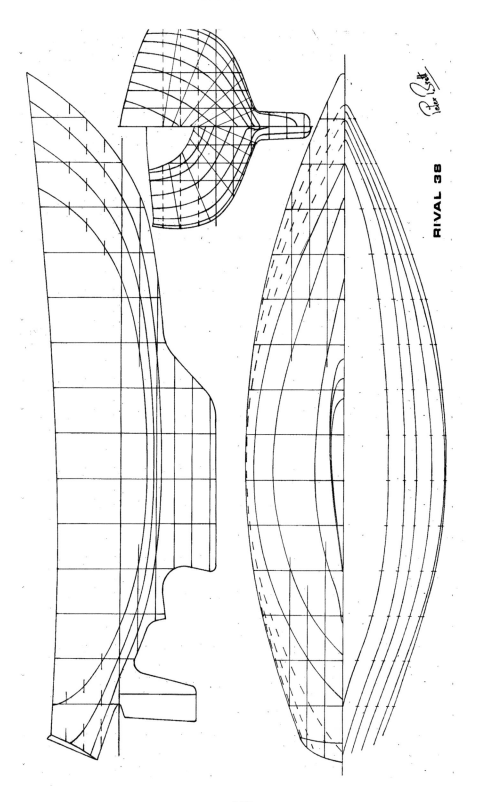

RIVAL 38

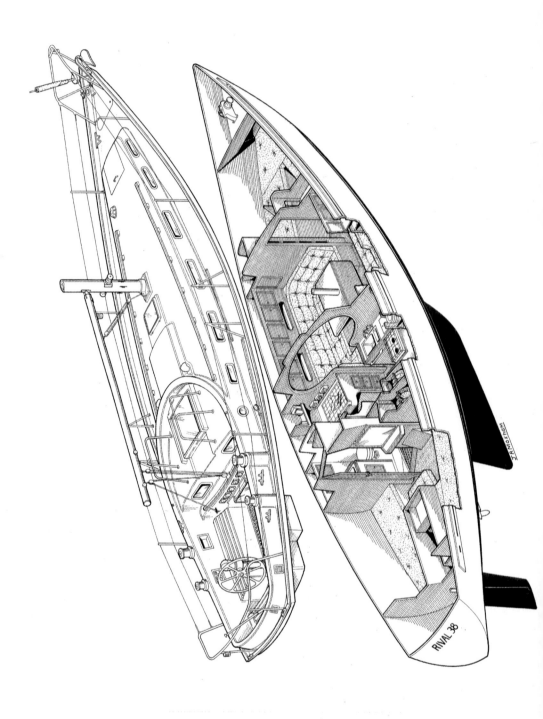

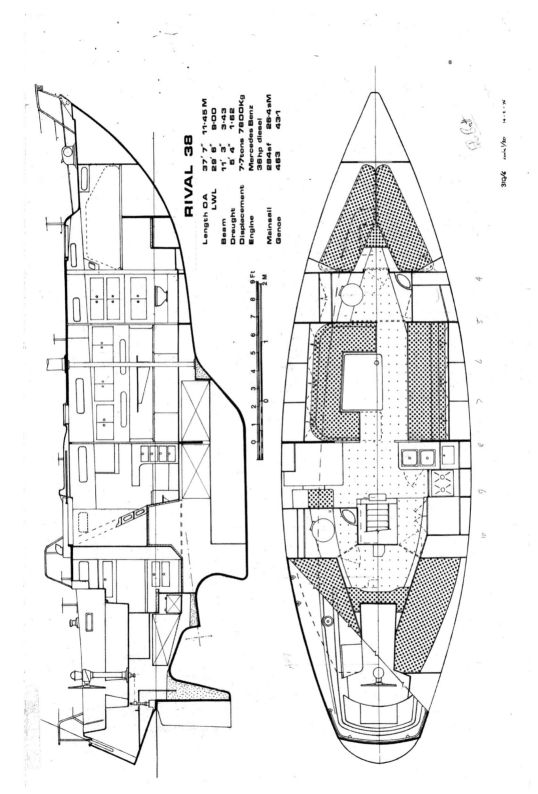

RIVAL 38

Length OA	37' 7"	11·45M
LWL	29' 6"	9·00
Beam	11' 3"	3·43
Draught	5' 4"	1·62
Displacement	7·7tons	7800Kg
Engine	Mercedes Benz	
	36hp diesel	
Mainsail	284sf	26·4sM
Genoa	463	43·1